OUT OF THE SEATS
AND INTO THE STREETS

RON DOTZLER

Out of the Seats and Into the Streets
Copyright © 2015 by Ron Dotzler

This book was written to encourage Christians to pursue a purposeful relationship with Jesus by getting out of the seats and into the streets. The stories shared in this book are true, though some names have been changed to protect the actual people.

Scripture quotations, as noted, come from these translations:

Holy Bible. New Living Translation. Copyright ©1996, 2004, 2007 by Tyndale House Foundation. Used by permission of Tyndale House Publishers, Inc., Carol Stream, Illinois 60188. All rights reserved.

New King James Version. Copyright © 1982 by Thomas Nelson. Used by permission. All rights reserved.

The Holy Bible, New International Version. Copyright © 1973, 1978, 1984, 2011 by Biblica, Inc. Used by permission. All rights reserved worldwide.

The Message. Copyright © 1993, 1994, 1995, 1996, 2000, 2001, 2002. Used by permission of NavPress Publishing Group.

For information, contact:
ABIDE · P.O. Box 11489 · Omaha, NE 68111
402-455-7807   www.abideomaha.org

Ghostwriter: Angela Welch Prusia
        www.angelawelchprusia.com
Cover design: Reynaldo Licayan
ISBN 978-1517147105

DEDICATION

This book is dedicated to my beautiful wife, Twany, and our fourteen wonderful children: Nekiesha, Makhoal, Jason, Jonathan, Joshua, Radiance, Myhiah, Jeremiah, Krehauna, Taylea, Saveenha, Casia, Josiah and Zhyael.

Mom and I have always dreamed of and worked toward the day each of you would become incredible world-changing leaders. Early on in our marriage, God made it very clear that whatever *good things* we would achieve would pale in comparison to how many *greater things* you, our children, would accomplish.

Our hope and prayer is for the truths contained in this book to elevate you, our children, to do *greater things* as you live fully surrendered to Jesus. May these words empower you to advance Christ's kingdom in the most compelling and complete way possible as you get out of the seats and into the streets.

The person who trusts me will not only do what I'm doing but even greater things . . .
John 14:12 MSG

WHAT PEOPLE ARE SAYING

"Inner city work can be difficult but Ron and Twany, a biracial couple, represent the hope of reconciliation. Their work in Omaha is producing incredible fruit—having developed a young multi-ethnic generation of leaders who are creating innovative pathways of transformation. The Dotzler's story is not only powerful, it ignites passion for change."

Steve Bell, Author, Speaker & Executive Vice President of Willow Creek Association

"Ron Dotzler is one of very few pastors in the United States to get beyond moral rhetoric to measurable results in bringing spiritual, social, and financial transformation to neighborhoods and communities. His story is engaging; his model and methods are biblically based, cross-culturally relevant, and pragmatically transferable. I highly recommend this book to any pastor or ministry leader looking to advance a credible gospel witness in an increasingly diverse and cynical society."

Dr. Mark DeYmaz, Founding Pastor
Mosaic Church of Central Arkansas;
President, Mosaix Global Network;
Author of *Building a Healthy Multi-ethnic Church*

"As a biracial couple, Ron and Twany's authentic leadership is helping move our churches forward in reconciliation and revitalization. Their city-transforming efforts are gaining momentum in a generation desperate for peace and hope. Read their wonderful story and join them in changing the world for Christ."

John Perkins, Cofounder CCDA;
Founder, John and Vera Mae Perkins Foundation
Jackson, Mississippi

"For 25 years, the Dotzler's ministry has provided hope, support and resources to families in Omaha's high poverty neighborhoods. Ron and Twany are trusted community leaders, partners and mentors. ABIDE believes Omaha is 'Better Together,' and we are better thanks to the leadership of the Dotzler family."

Omaha Mayor Jean Stothert

"Ron and Twany are a tour de force for justice, compassion and love in Omaha. Out of the Seats and Into the Streets is much more than a saying for the Dotzlers. It is a passion, a lifestyle and a movement. Our church is dramatically different because of our partnership with ABIDE and Bridge. Dive in, and your life will be transformed, too!"

Mark Ashton, Lead Pastor
Christ Community Church, Omaha
Christian Missionary Alliance

"Ron Dotzler has been a valued partner with the Omaha Police Department over the last five years. This partnership has resulted in a reduction in crime in many of the neighborhoods where OPD and ABIDE collaborate. Ron's commitment to serving others is highlighted by his efforts to create stable neighborhoods, block by block. Ron and ABIDE work tirelessly to improve the community through ministering and community outreach. 'Better Together' is more than a mere motto, and truly exemplifies the manner in which he aims to improve the community for all."

Police Chief Todd Schmaderer
Omaha Police Department

"Ron and Twany have impacted my life, Young Life Omaha, and the life of West Hills Church profoundly. They embody true kingdom values, igniting others to see what God can do when the church truly joins hearts and hands together. They are truly two of my heroes. I know you will be blessed by the story of their lives and their amazing heart for ministry that is truly changing the city of Omaha for God's glory!"

Pam Moore, National Director of Training
Young Life
Denver, Colorado

"Ron and Twany Dotzler are examples of believers who are sold out to impacting a community for Christ. Their sacrifices to lift others is a daily reminder of the Commission left for the church. I pray this book will motivate others to leave their comfort zones and be a part of changing our communities for the better."

Pastor Selwyn Q. Bachus
Salem Baptist Church, Omaha

"We often pray, 'Thy Kingdom come, Thy will be done, on earth as it is in heaven.' This is a great prayer to pray! But what does it look like when the kingdom of God comes to a city? Ron and Twany Dotzler can tell you. Through 25 years of trial and error, they have discovered the bridge that brings the kingdom of God to the inner city through the local church. My paradigm to reaching our city has been challenged and changed because of their journey. And our partnership with them has challenged our church to 'get out of the seats and into the streets!' Get ready to be inspired and equipped to reach your city for God.'

Walt DeVries, Lead Pastor
Glad Tidings Church, Omaha
Assembly of God

"I have observed and played a small part in God taking a mixed couple from a corporate setting and transplanting them in the inner city with one of the highest crime rates in America. The love, vision and passion for ministry and breaking down walls enabled them to bring together blacks, whites and Latinos along with resources to establish a little heaven on earth with an Azusa Street type unity. They have radically impacted the lives of young people in the inner city where drugs, gang violence, sex and prison life no longer control their future. The Dotzlers have actually succeeded where others have failed in meeting the needs of the lost in the inner city. This is a model of God's love that is working."

Pastor Robert Hall
Cathedral of Love
Church of God in Christ (C.O.G.I.C.)

"What God has done in North Omaha through the ministry of Ron and Twany Dotzler is both incredible and inspirational. When they said, 'Here am I, send me,' years ago and moved their comfortable, suburban lives to a hurting inner city, they could not have predicted how many thousands of people they would touch through the formation of ABIDE and the planting of Bridge Church. They have changed a city and changed my life deeply. For that I'm grateful."

Dr. Steve Holdaway, Lead Pastor
LifeSpring Church; Bellevue, Nebraska
Southern Baptist Convention

"I've often thought, 'Why do we tell so many stories of impact that happened a century ago and few from our own era?' One of the rare and profound exceptions is the astounding 'God story' of Ron and Twany Dotzler. They did and continue to do the outrageous by leaving the American dream, which was in their possession, to embrace a dream of inspiring ordinary Christians, by their radical example to get out of the safety of their church seats and into the adventure of the city streets. Like Hudson Taylor or David Livingstone of old is the modern, inspiring and livable story of Ron, Twany and ABIDE. Read at your own risk! You may find yourself leaving your safe seats to experience God, in the streets of your own city."

Les Beauchamp, Lead Pastor
LifeGate Church, Omaha

"Most of us buy into the notion to never put all of our eggs into one basket. Ron and Twany put all of their eggs into one basket, then gave the basket to the Lord. We who know them and the work of ABIDE and Bridge will never be the same."

Bill Bowers,
Presbyterian Pastor

"Ron and Twany empower pastors in their calling, unite congregations in mission, build bridges between neighborhoods, form community in the midst of chaos, and relentlessly and joyfully invite Christians to 'get out of the seats and into the streets.' For Ron and Twany, 'out of the seats and into the streets' isn't just a slogan, it's an unstoppable drive. Their ministry in our city has resulted in churches from across our community and from diverse denominational backgrounds to unite in being a witness for Christ together. Dundee Presbyterian Church is more faithful in its stewardship of the gospel due in no small part to the ministry and hearts of the Dotzlers and their amazing team. If vision, humility, steadfastness, and love were salt water, Ron, Twany, ABIDE, and Bridge would be the Pacific Ocean."

Pastor Bob Jordan
Dundee Presbyterian Church, Omaha

"Ron and Twany Dotzler don't just talk. Yes, they do talk, and as they do, they inspire, teach and motivate. But for them, it's never stopped there. They live out everything they say. For over 25 years, I've been privileged to watch their journey from the suburbs to their amazing work in the inner city, taking risks and making what many would consider, radical moves with their family. This book chronicles that journey. It will inspire you to put action behind your faith. The Dotzlers are mobilizers. This book WILL mobilize you, just as the title says!"

Pastor Lincoln Murdoch, Executive Director
Step Up To Life

CONTENTS

SECTION I: OUT OF THE SEATS

WHEN GOD GETS OUR **ATTENTION**

WHEN GOD GRABS OUR **AFFECTION**

WHEN GOD CALLS US TO **ACTION**

SECTION II: INTO THE STREETS

ADOPTING NEIGHBORHOODS

BRIDGE CHURCHES

INVEST IN LEADERS

DIVERSITY

ENGAGE PARTNERS

SECTION I:
OUT OF THE SEATS

WHEN GOD GETS OUR
ATTENTION

PLAYING IT SAFE

LATE NIGHT CONFRONTATION

Standing on a street corner an hour before midnight in the heart of the inner city wasn't my first choice for Friday night fun. But when a group from a partnering church wanted a lesson on prayer, I knew of no better place. Praying on site for insight meant getting out of the church seats and into the streets.

A young man took notice of one of the ladies in our group and lumbered toward her like someone on a drug high. His wiry frame and unkempt afro contrasted with her petite size.

"Hey. How's it going?" I approached the corner of 30th and Ames in an attempt to diffuse the situation.

The young man jerked in my direction and snarled in disgust. "White boy, what're you doing in my community?" Alcohol tainted the air and slurred his words.

Fear shone from the young lady's eyes. I nodded toward our group, and she slowly backed away.

"You need to leave," he spat at me. "White boys don't belong here."

A car rolled past, buoyed with hydraulics and bass thumping. Despite the late hour, the place teemed with young people dressed for a night of clubbing. Streetlights spilled over the activity, revealing various faces in the crowd. At least the noise would drown out any confrontation. An audience would only fuel the young man's ego.

"You got some money?"

I shook my head.

"Don't lie to me, white boy." He got in my face. "I got no respect for liars."

Red lines crisscrossed the whites of his eyes. He was too strung out on drugs. An argument would only escalate matters.

"See that building?" He nodded behind him toward a run-down structure known for its reputation as a crack house. "That's my home. But you white boys live in big fancy places, so I know you have money."

I didn't tell him I'd moved to north Omaha nearly a decade earlier. The inner city had become my home.

My silence agitated the young man further. "You white people are the reason us black people got it so hard."

Sweat beaded on my lip. His accusation singled me out as the enemy. "Help me, Jesus." I breathed a silent prayer.

Profanity spewed from his mouth. "I should pop you right now."

I took a step back, and the movement infuriated him.

"You trying to get away from me?" He closed the distance between us, ready to throw a punch. "Think you're too good for a black brother?"

I gulped in a vain effort to push down my rising fear. "Please protect me, Jesus." I prayed like crazy. I had ten kids and a wife who needed me.

"I'm going to blast you with a cap, white boy." He shook as his screams reached a fever pitch. "Give me money now, or kiss your sorry life goodbye."

He reached into his pocket for a gun. My heart thudded in panic. I couldn't outrun a bullet.

"God, help me."

I was a dead man.

VELVEETAVILLE

I am white, and my wife is black. I was born and raised in a small rural town in Iowa with a booming population of 300 white people. My wife, on the other hand, was born and raised in an urban black section of the Washington, D.C., metropolitan area with over 5 million people.

We met in college, married, started a family, and lived a comfortable Christian life. We attended church several times a week and read our Bibles, all the while amassing houses, cars, and other possessions in some vain attempt to "keep up with the Joneses," whoever they were.

Before life in the inner city came life in Velveetaville, the place where I was being processed by my culture. The more money I made the more I spent improving my family's lifestyle.

My net worth, according to suburbology, equaled the sum total of the things I attained and the accolades I achieved. A never-ending cycle of need and greed dominated my life. In five short years as a chemical engineer, I fattened my family's financial portfolio on my quest toward "success."

Make more money. Buy more stuff. I bought into the culture's mantra and came out as processed as my next door neighbor.

Make more money. Buy more stuff.

Make more money. Buy more stuff.

I lived on an assembly line in a suburb called Velveetaville. My culture mass-produced thousands of people just like me blindly following the American dream. Two pieces of bread— enjoyment and comfort—sandwiched my processed cheese life. The only difference between my neighbor and me was that he didn't attend my Sunday morning club called church.

Because I followed Christ, I justified my comfortable lifestyle. After all, wasn't I just enjoying God's blessings as I prepared for my family's future?

I didn't consider myself materialistic or absorbed in conformity, and yet, my bank account and lifestyle proved otherwise. God's dream for my life was not my pursuit. The American dream had somehow swallowed me up.

Without realizing it, I'd built a cocoon of protection that insulated my family from a broken and dangerous world. I'd prepared my family for financial success so that nothing could penetrate the safety net surrounding us.

Satisfaction eluded me. Outside of my family, friends and career, I longed for a greater sense of purpose in my life. While I'd heard people talk about knowing God's calling for their lives, I'd never experienced that reality. Something was missing.

Life in the suburbs isolated me from the harsh reality of many in my city. When I read newspaper articles about murder and crime in north Omaha, I critically judged "those people" for their irresponsibility and blamed "them" for what they should or should not be doing. In my negative view, I thought "they" deserved the mess of problems they were experiencing.

The inner city statistics were alarming. High crime, violence and murder seemed normal. Poor education, high unemployment, dilapidated houses and unkempt yards left little to be desired.

Because of my cynicism, the distance between me and "them" left me unmoved and unaffected. Quite sadly, I felt no compassion or concern. I never gave time or money to help the inner city. I was clueless to the conditions impacting a large population of children, youth and families.

Velveetaville left me yearning for more. God had a lot of work to do in order to change my cold and calloused heart.

PLAYING IT SAFE

With the growing emptiness I felt in Velveetaville, God piqued my attention. My faith was summed up in a Christian tract on a table in a public building. The booklet instructed a new Christian how to live: "Now that you've given your life to Jesus, read the Bible, pray, go to church and do good."

The stark contrast between this "nice" version of Christianity and the Christianity of the Bible stopped me. The description of a Christian on the tract seemed nothing like the portrayal of early followers of Jesus found in the New Testament.

Early Christians made a difference. Followers of Jesus defended the cause of the poor and the needy. The church fed widows and helped orphans. Christians set cities in uproar and changed economies. Paul's teaching in Ephesus convicted sorcerers to burn their scrolls and challenged silversmiths to stop creating shrines for the local gods. Believers sold all their possessions and lived completely devoted to Jesus. They were willing to give their lives to advance God's kingdom.

These early Christians turned the world upside down. Sadly, my version of Christianity was more like the tract than the New Testament.

Ouch.

The more I studied the early Christians, the more I realized my view of Christianity was incomplete. Early disciples had more than conviction. They had a passion and direction that compelled them to sacrifice so others could find hope. Jesus radically impacted their lives. This, in turn, radically changed their cities . . . and ultimately, impacted the world.

Before Jesus died and commissioned His followers to spread the good news, He looked upon Jerusalem and wept. His heart broke for the city.

Did I have the same compassion for my city? Questions began to enter my mind and heart like never before. God wanted my attention. Sitting in a church pew wasn't enough.

Did the pain and suffering in the inner city break my heart?

Did I weep for my neighbors?

2

THE POWER OF PERSONAL AWAKENING

MY SISTER'S DEATH

Growing up, my faith was the faith of my parents. I enjoyed attending church every Sunday until college when I no longer saw the need. Even though I would tell you I was a Christian, I didn't think much about God or His plan for my life.

When my older sister, Lois, was diagnosed with a rare cancer at age 27, I didn't realize the extent of the disease. I was a free spirit living the party life in college. The distance between her home in Kansas City and my home at Tarkio College in Missouri shielded me from the ravaging effect of her two-year battle. When my mom rallied us kids around Lois the week before her death, I was dumbfounded at the change. Skin clung to my sister's bones. Lois had dropped to 40 pounds.

"It's time to say goodbye." My mom nudged me into my sister's bedroom. Her two toddlers played in the living room with my other siblings.

I couldn't find the words to speak. I'd never been confronted with death. Fear rendered me helpless.

"How're you doing, Ronnie?" my sweet sister broke the awkwardness. She'd always been my biggest encourager. *How could she be so strong, even in the face of death?*

Mom and Lois talked while my skin crawled. I had to get out of the room. Guys weren't supposed to show emotion, and I was a wreck.

A week later, the call came in the early hours of the morning.

"Lois died," my sister Mary broke the news.

I collapsed on the floor in my dorm room. Lois couldn't be dead. She was so young.

The funeral broke me. Death gripped everyone who jammed into the small Catholic church. I followed the procession to the cemetery and watched as my sister's casket was lowered into the ground.

Death haunted me with unanswered questions.

What happened after death? Was there more to life than what I saw with my eyes? Did my life have purpose?

A WAKE UP CALL

My brother Ray tried to talk to me about Jesus, but his words made no sense. I returned to college and immersed myself in the party scene to forget.

God got my attention less than a month later. Drunk and exhausted after Greek Week, I decided to rest at Ray's house.

Despite my weary state, I left the party around midnight. Midpoint into the two-hour trip, I rolled down the window to stay alert. Gulping fresh air only helped for a few seconds. I slapped my face and sang in my loudest voice, but nothing helped.

The glare of headlights and the blare of a horn jolted me awake. An oncoming car was headed straight for me. I jerked the wheel and barely missed a wreck. I looked over and saw the clock. It read 2:08.

I should have pulled over. Instead, I drifted off to sleep eight or nine more times over the next hour, only to be awakened just in time to regain control of the car and miss a head-on collision with an oncoming car, bridge or ditch. Somehow, I made it to my brother's house where I crashed on the couch.

The next morning my brother jostled me awake. "Ron, Ron, are you okay?"

My head pounded. "Yeah, I'm okay. Why?"

Ray pushed my shoulder. "God woke me up at 2:08 to pray for you."

His words broke through my fog. My jaw dropped.

The idea of a personal God was foreign to me. The big guy seemed distant and invisible. But my brother seemed to think Jesus was his best friend. The way he described Jesus made me wonder if he'd seen the dude with his own eyes. Ray explained that he'd had a radical experience with Jesus, but I still didn't understand. All I knew was that suddenly my brother couldn't get enough Jesus, or church, or Bible study.

Now I couldn't help but wonder. *If Jesus woke up my brother to pray for me, could God be real? Did He have a plan for my life?*

I stayed with Ray and his wife for the summer in Omaha and worked. He invited me to go to church with them on Sundays, so I agreed.

Each Sunday I heard the pastor share about Jesus in a way that seemed real. One particular morning, a Chinese woman named Nora Lam shared her story, and Jesus got a hold of my heart. I couldn't believe the woman had been miraculously pregnant for 12 months while working in a labor camp. God answered her prayers to slow the baby's arrival until the two found safety. God's intervention amazed me, yet He'd done the same in my life. If God hadn't alerted my brother to pray, I'd be dead. The realization made me shudder. When the woman asked if anyone wanted to surrender his or her life to Jesus, I raised my hand. Peace flooded my emptiness.

Returning to college, God began a radical change in my life. I quit drinking, stepped down from my role as fraternity president, and started leading Bible studies. I didn't know the difference between the Old and New Testament, but I earned a new reputation: Jesus freak.

WHY DOES SKIN COLOR MATTER?

During this time, I fell in love with a beautiful African-American woman named Twany. When she became a Christian as well, I couldn't wait to spend the rest of my life with her. Though I considered myself colorblind in regard to our interracial relationship, God revealed my cultural blind spots that skewed both my view of life and Christianity.

When I took Twany back to my small town in Iowa, love and naivety blinded me. I assumed everyone loved my African-American wife. Years later, my mother told me I caused quite the uproar in the all-white town.

A huge surprise came when I called Twany's parents to ask for her hand in marriage. Her mother's adamant refusal both shocked and confused me. *What did she have against me? Had Twany's mother seen my picture and didn't like what she saw? Did she know how poor I really was as a college student?*

"But why?" I got up the nerve to ask.

"Because you are white." She didn't even hesitate.

White? What did color have to do with anything? I was totally confused. Classifications in rural Iowa broke down to male or female, Catholic or non-Catholic, even German or Swedish, but never white. Generally, I understood everyone around me as American. This kind of color language was completely unfamiliar to me—as foreign as a second language. *Why did color matter?*

With passion and pursuit, I somehow convinced my in-laws to bless our marriage, but I soon recognized my new wife held the same cautious edge her parents had about white people.

When I dared to call Twany prejudiced, she immediately fired back, telling me how prejudiced I was toward blacks. Her response sounded defensive to me, so I asked for proof. *Didn't my choice to marry a black woman show my true beliefs?*

Twany couldn't give me specific examples of my prejudice, but that didn't change her mind. She was convinced I was prejudiced.

On the contrary, I had plenty of examples of her prejudice toward whites. At a play at the Orpheum Theater in Omaha, Twany pointed out only five black people were present in the audience. "What?" I didn't hide my irritation at her constant awareness of race. "Why would you say that? Are you the black monitor?"

Whenever we shopped together, Twany would point out how closely the sales clerks watched her. No matter what I said, she fell back on her past training to "watch out for Charlie," a saying in the black community to beware of white people.

Twany justified her opinions, interpreting her responses in light of her past racial experiences.

Frustration built inside me.

God had me in His crosshairs. He used my love for Twany to get my attention. Again.

BEING BLACK IN WHITE AMERICA

Visiting my in-laws for the first time in Washington, D.C., put me in unfamiliar territory.

Everyone around me was black—an entirely new and somewhat uncomfortable experience for me. Until then, I'd never really considered skin color.

Being the minority forced me to see life through a totally different context, but I still had a hard time understanding what my in-laws meant by being *black* in *white* America.

They talked about their experiences sitting at the back of the bus and drinking from designated water fountains. They couldn't eat at certain restaurants or get particular jobs simply because of the color of their skin. Even attending a Catholic school in their suburban area was out of the question because they were black.

My wife described her experience being part of the only black family on a club swim team. White kids ridiculed and spit on Twany's older siblings while their coaches did nothing. Little changed when she joined. Some white parents would discipline their children because they'd allowed a black teammate to beat them in a swim race even though they belonged to the same team. Twany's siblings qualified for the Pan Am Games, but couldn't participate because there were no facilities for blacks. Other blacks mocked them for participating with whites. Twany and her siblings felt alone, outsiders no matter where they turned.

I AM PREJUDICED

I interpreted their experiences through the filter of my rural white upbringing, so I was skeptical. Surely my wife and her parents were exaggerating. *Didn't all Americans have the same opportunities and realities?*

No matter how many times my wife reminded me of her family's history of inequality, I still felt she was being overly prejudiced toward white people.

"It's unfair to lump every white person together," I told her on many occasions. "You're the one who's prejudiced. Not me."

I was frustrated and angry that my wife always insinuated that I, as a "white" person, was responsible for slavery and injustice. I didn't understand why she connected me to the suffering and injustice that took place years before my birth. I didn't commit the atrocities. Why should I take the blame? In my mind, if I could prove that I wasn't prejudiced, she couldn't attach me to the inequalities and horrors of the black experience in America.

One night as we sat in our car in the driveway, I reveled in the beauty and blessing of our firstborn daughter Kiesha who was about three months old. While she sat in her car seat between my wife and me, I envisioned Kiesha's future as a godly woman who would one day become a missionary and marry a white guy.

"Not my daughter." Twany shook her head. "Our daughter is going to marry a black guy."

"What?" My eyes bugged out. "You've got to be kidding. My daughter's going to marry a white guy."

An argument immediately broke out.

We went back and forth, debating whether our daughter would marry a white or a black guy.

Twany glared at me, finally cornering me. "See, I knew you were prejudiced!"

There it was.

I couldn't believe what I'd just said.

My words revealed my heart. I was truly prejudiced, and I couldn't deny it.

PREFERENCES AND PREJUDICE

After calming down, my wife and I had a long conversation about how our internal preferences often led to our prejudices. Whether intentional or not, these preferences conditioned us to make certain decisions without much thought.

My comment about my daughter marrying a white guy reflected my internal preferences based on my rural white cultural conditioning. I had an incomplete perspective that had been tainted by my life experiences. Many times I would talk about the "good old days," and my wife would fire back, "For who? We were in slavery back then." Years of living alongside other whites made me comfortable in the white zone. I wasn't being mean-spirited or intentionally unjust; rather I'd responded from cultural conditioning.

Admitting my prejudice helped me understand how my wife and her family, as well as a whole population of people, were marginalized and withheld from fully participating in the broader society's opportunities. Hearing their first-hand accounts of injustice hit me like a punch in the gut. These realities didn't end with slavery. They continued to affect many families of color today.

The playing field was not level. A "glass ceiling" stunted the potential of many minorities. Hard work and ethical behavior weren't enough to overcome overwhelming hurdles of injustice. Without leverage or help from concerned people, these obstacles loomed as insurmountable barriers.

The same was true of my Christianity. My preferences influenced my decision-making and guided my interactions. If I wasn't intentional and fully committed to preferring others above myself, my natural preferences dictated my choices. I got too easily distracted by keeping up with the Joneses in Velveetaville and forgot about the rest of the world God wanted me to love.

Because of the differences between my upbringing and Twany's experiences, God got my attention and widened my limited view of Christianity. He cleared my tainted glasses and began to show me people through the lens of His love. By using diversity, God wanted me to find ways to get past the familiar and develop intentional habits that showed love and justice to everyone, including those unlike me. For this to happen, I definitely needed to make some changes.

CHAPTER

3

CHANGE

ESCAPING VELVEETAVILLE

Fast forward a decade.

Despite my heavy involvement at church, I couldn't shake the growing unrest inside me. Leading rural outreaches and Bible studies no longer fulfilled me. Something was missing. I had to talk to my pastor.

"I feel unsettled," I confided in the man who I'd come to respect. His teaching and leadership had helped ground me in God's word. "Pastor, I feel like I need to go to the mission field."

"Ron, you have a great family and a wonderful job. You adopted the twins, and you do more ministry than most pastors I know." He smiled. "Keep doing what you're doing."

I followed his advice for the next few months, but my discontent only grew. My life had to count for more than the sum total of my family, my career, and my church attendance.

I met my pastor again. "I can't do this anymore."

I had to escape Velveetaville.

My wife and I assumed God wanted us to join the foreign mission field, so after much prayer, we made a radical decision to serve overseas. I quit my job as a chemical engineer, and we sold everything—houses, cars and a truck-load of possessions.

With growing excitement and a new sense of adventure, Twany and I searched the newspaper after our house sold. We would live anywhere in Omaha while we prepared to move overseas.

Except the inner city. North Omaha was off limits, not even an option.

Relocating to a third world country was more appealing than moving to the inner city—a dangerous, dilapidated, hopeless place. North Omaha was far too unsafe to raise five children all under the age of five.

Apparently, God had other ideas.

ROACH TRAUMA

Moving to the inner city came by accident. Property owners in the suburbs were reluctant to rent to our large family when they heard our short timeline. The chance to find a rental house in the safer neighborhoods of Omaha never materialized. God wanted us out of Velveetaville, but He had somewhere closer than Africa in mind.

A man I'd met through leading rural outreaches offered us free rent in exchange for removing illegal squatters and fixing up his place. The catch: the home was in the inner city. Against our desires and better judgment, we moved into a 700 square-foot, two-bedroom home infested with roaches.

Having come from rural Iowa, I'd seen my share of wildlife, including rodents and insects, but never had I experienced roaches like this before. Their brown exoskeletons were everywhere, covering each wall, floor and ceiling.

Prior to moving, family and friends had helped us prepare the house by cleaning and exterminating the pests. Despite our measures, the roaches only seemed to multiply.

Roaches skittered over our clothes, bedded in our dresser drawers, and showed up in every place imaginable. To my horror, my children entertained themselves by counting the number of roaches running across the basement floor. The pests were dirty, disgusting and indestructible.

Multiple exterminators explained the difficulty of removing our roaches because of our neighbors' infestation. No matter what the experts did, the pests would migrate from one house to another. We could never be roach-free. The news devastated me. Roaches were crawling through my nightmares. I felt like an unwilling participant in a low-budget horror film.

The presence of our pests overwhelmed me to the point of obsession. One particular night as our family arrived home, I ran into the house ahead of everyone, grabbed a flyswatter, flipped on the lights, and started killing roaches. They crunched under my feet and splattered against my plastic weapon, their oozing guts making me want to vomit.

I couldn't overpower them. Hordes of roaches covered the walls, the stove, the sink, everywhere I looked. Within seconds, I'd killed 72 from their rank. Counting them was madness. Stress from roach trauma sent me to the brink of a mental breakdown.

My mission to kill *every* roach in the Dotzler household had failed. The roaches had won.

That night, as my wife and I lay on our pull-out sleeper sofa in the living room, our roach problem overwhelmed me. I'd finally come to the end of my rope.

As I looked into my wife's eyes, exhausted and desperate, I realized I'd done everything except pray. The idea was an afterthought, something I'd never considered.

Our prayer was simple yet desperate. Twany and I could do nothing. Our roach problem needed God's intervention. Only He could transform our miserable conditions.

The next morning, I couldn't believe it. The house was roach-free. In fact, we never saw another roach the remaining two years we lived in the house. I was dumbfounded. Gratitude and excitement bubbled deep inside me. A simple, desperate prayer had led to an incredible miracle. When I finally gave up, God showed up. He got my attention once again by proving He cared about every detail in my life.

Independence had been ingrained in me from a young age. Becoming an engineer had required hard work and discipline. When I became a Christian, I approached Bible study with the same determination and grit, but countless hours of Bible studies and sermons never prepared me for my new world.

Life on another planet would've been easier than life in the inner city. I couldn't fix the crushing problems of poverty and violence any more than I could fix my roach problem. I needed God more than ever.

WHITE PEOPLE
CAN'T BE CHRISTIAN

Our first priority was to get to know people in the community by serving at local churches. Whereas Twany had been one of the few African-Americans at our church in the suburbs, now I was the minority in the inner city churches. To my surprise, an older African-American woman at one Baptist church laughingly confided in me, "White people can't be Christian."

Her statement shocked me to the core. I couldn't believe what I'd just heard. *How could she make such a blanket statement?* She had to be joking. Surely this woman didn't think I was headed to hell. Her statement definitely got my attention, but I couldn't help but wonder if I had missed the punch line.

For once, I didn't know what to say. In a half-hearted sense of curiosity and dismissal, I kept silent and smiled.

A few days later, another African-American woman pronounced the same sentiment. "You know, Ron, white people can't be Christian."

The same bluntness surprised me. According to my rural upbringing, being forthright was considered a sign of disrespect. The black church experience, however, was filled with a level of emotion that opened me to a deeper emotional reality in my life. When I began to let go of inhibitions and expressed my true feelings, I was discovering a new level of freedom.

My curiosity made me bold. *Why would these women feel this way?* With as much sensitivity as possible, and a certain level of fear and intimidation, I treaded potential racial tension to ask this woman if she would talk with me. I had to understand the meaning behind her words. As she would fully explain, this statement was a common understanding in the African-American community with an experiential basis of truth.

Deep conviction and obvious passion underscored her beliefs while personal experiences cemented her stance. Hands waving and eyes flashing, she painted a picture of growing up in a life of poverty. Every night as a little girl, her mother would read from the Bible before she slept.

From these early memories to her regular involvement in church, this woman had heard with profound clarity what the Bible had to say about how Christians treated the poor and the needy. She recalled white people moving out when her family moved into a neighborhood. These experiences, which were deeply embedded in her heart and mind, shaped her beliefs.

In 52 years, this woman had never seen a white person come into her inner city community to help her in her time of need. "Some might blow in, blow up and blow out, but never would they live in my community," she said. In fact, I challenged her thinking because I was serving alongside her as the first white person she'd known to really live in and get involved in her community.

WAS I TRULY A CHRISTIAN?

The more this woman and other African-Americans described their experiences to me, the more I questioned my own Christianity. *Did verifiable actions back my beliefs? What evidence showed my identity in Christ? Was I truly a Christian?*

I thought I had all the right beliefs about God, but I had to agree with these women. An honest look at my life showed I hadn't lived out my faith in real ways. No wonder they believed white people couldn't be Christians. As a whole, I, as a white person sitting in church, had a lot of words, but very few deeds.

Apparently, God's favorite classroom was beyond the confines of the sanctuary and the Sunday school classroom. Experiencing a personal relationship with Jesus was only the first step. Through racial diversity and life in the inner city,

God was definitely getting my attention in ways I hadn't expected. If His lessons came with bullet points, the following proved true in my life:

- My view of Christianity was skewed and incomplete.
- I was prejudiced. My experiences had shaped me.
- I was too independent and self-absorbed.
- I didn't really live out my faith. I had a lot of talk but little action to back up my beliefs.
- God got my attention because I needed to change.

Now came the real test. Once God had my attention, He wanted my affection. Would I love my new neighbors, no matter the cost?

WHEN GOD GRABS OUR **AFFECTION**

CHAPTER

4

PRAYING ALMOST KILLED ME

BEGGING GOD FOR MY LIFE

I was a dead man.

I'd come to pray for the inner city, and in an ironic twist, I was begging God for my life. The young man standing inches from me reached into his pocket for a gun. My heart thudded in panic. I couldn't outrun a bullet.

"God, help me."

The seconds ticked by, feeling like an eternity. I stood at the corner of 30th and Ames as the world around me came to a standstill. The last moments of my life played out in agonizing torture.

Every fiber within me cried out for help as the young man dug around his pocket for his weapon. "Please save me, God."

A voice broke through my panic. "Ron, you will not die." The slightest pause felt like a beat in a screenplay. "Until I'm finished with you."

Peace flooded me. God had a plan for my life.

The young man grew frustrated with his search. He pulled his hand from his pocket and stared at his empty palm in bewilderment.

I couldn't believe it. Without another word, he simply walked off. The confrontation was over. Exhaustion, relief and gratitude overwhelmed me.

I wouldn't die until Jesus was finished with me.

The revelation hit me, awakening me to God's power over my life. True safety was only within the hands of Jesus.

Through this near-death confrontation, I cried out to God, and He answered my prayer. This encounter brought me to a new level of dependence and submission in my relationship with Jesus Christ. This new realization compelled me to dig deeper about living life with passion and purpose.

No amount of classroom teaching or Sunday morning preaching on prayer could have impacted me like this experience. My desperation showed my dependence on God. I needed Him like never before. God shapes us into the people He desires us to become through "out of the seat" experiences in unfamiliar and uncomfortable environments where we need God.

This experience reminded me of a conversation where I once asked a pastor friend from Mexico what he thought of American Christians. His response floored me. "You Christians in the

United States have no need for God because you think you can do it all on your own."

Wow. What a statement.

His words struck home as God used my new inner city neighborhood to uncover my self-focused and self-reliant tendencies. While I imagined God using me to transform the brokenness of the inner city, God was actually using the brokenness of the inner city to transform me. He not only had my attention, He was grabbing my affection.

WHEN GOD IS COMFORTABLE

My discomfort not only awakened my dependence on God, it taught me that God is comfortable when I'm uncomfortable. Being in uncomfortable places increased my reliance on God. I had to trust Him rather than myself, something that made me extremely uncomfortable, but made God very comfortable. I needed Jesus to show up in ways I never considered necessary. To lean into Christ's supernatural abilities meant admitting my own inabilities.

My desperation placed me exactly where God wanted me. Working hard at living the Christian life wasn't enough. My independence didn't allow

God to work. I needed to step aside and trust Him to make a way in seemingly impossible situations. As John the Baptist said in John 3:30, "He must increase, but I must decrease." (NKJV) The intersection of faith and dependence on God was truly the place of miracles.

I couldn't control when I would die, but I could control for whom I would live and how I chose to do so. Choosing Jesus meant accepting the dual reality of not only "dying for Christ" but also "living for Christ."

Temporary comfort wasn't worth the cost. Living with discomfort, in light of being available for God to use me, was real faith. Living within the comfort of my own self-reliance left out the power of Jesus. Living *uncomfortably* would bring real transformation.

The inner city wrecked my heart. The first time I saw my neighbors across the street, a man ran out of the house yelling and carrying a machete while another man chased him with a pitchfork. The police visited my new neighbors more times in one week than I'd seen their presence in all my years living in the suburbs. In a strange combination, an abundance of drug addicts, prostitutes, and gang members lived alongside laborers, daycare providers, and teachers who made up my block.

The dysfunction in my inner city neighborhood was like nothing I'd experienced. The constant gunfire, crime, violence and poverty took on new meaning when I began to meet my neighbors.

North Omaha was no longer a faceless community I read about in the newspaper. The daily trauma awakened me to the pain God felt and increased my empathy. God moved beyond getting my attention to grabbing my affection for my hurting neighbors.

COVERED IN BLOOD

A well-known drug dealer named Markus lived next door to us. He wanted nothing to do with God the first time we met, so we talked about other topics long past midnight.

Two nights later, our family returned home late after visiting friends. After putting the kids to sleep in the two bedrooms, Twany and I pulled out the sleeper sofa in the living room, which became our bedroom at night, and settled into bed.

A knock startled me. Anxiety gripped me as I headed for the front door. Without a porch light or peephole, I couldn't see who waited outside our home.

"Honey, pray," I told Twany.

Slowly opening the door, I blinked in disbelief. My drug-dealing neighbor stood in front of me covered in blood.

Fear made my voice tremble. "What's going on, Markus?"

"Ron, you're the only friend I have in the world."

I couldn't decide what shocked me more—the circumstance or the admission. We'd only just met. Surely I couldn't be his only friend in the world.

"Will you come over?" Markus asked. "I need to talk to you before I kill myself."

His words left me reeling in disbelief and shock. The comfortable life I once lived in the suburbs was a far cry from the chaos that plagued the reality of my neighbors.

What would Jesus do? The phrase sounded above all other thoughts of violence and crime.

"Let me change, and I'll come over."

This young man's incredible despair and hopelessness tested me. I needed to help, but I had no clue what to do. *What in the world was I thinking?*

I switched my pajamas for clothes and explained the situation to Twany. Before I left, I repeated my earlier request, "Honey, pray."

Upheaval met my eyes as I approached Markus' house. Remnants of a domestic dispute were everywhere. Glass littered the ground. The windshield on his girlfriend's car had been shattered along with several windows in the house. The front door had been ripped off its hinges. Torn clothes and broken furniture covered the front lawn. The place was a disaster.

Inside the house, I sidestepped broken picture frames and pieces of a baby's crib. Markus sat on what remained of an old couch, bloody hands covering his face. Blood streaked his pale flesh like war paint. Long matted bangs stuck to his skin.

"What's going on?" I sat next to him.

"My girlfriend and I got into a fight." Markus exhaled. "She took off, so you need to know some things before I kill myself."

KEN ANDERSON

A LIFE AND DEATH CONVERSATION

His words rang through my head. I'd never talked to someone so desperate. *Why would someone choose death? Didn't everyone have opportunities to improve life circumstances? What about hope?*

I had no clue what to say or do. I made myself available, but my comfort zone had long since exploded.

"God has a wonderful plan for your life," I interrupted Markus as he started listing reasons why he needed to commit suicide. "Killing yourself is not the answer."

I didn't know what else to say, so I asked if I could pray for him.

"Okay," he grunted.

I put my arm around him and offered God an urgent, heartfelt prayer.

After I finished praying, Markus picked up right where he'd left off, telling me to let his girlfriend know he had a gun stashed between the mattresses. He wanted me to talk to her and his parents after he killed himself.

"God has a plan for your life," I repeated. "Killing yourself is not the answer." Like before,

I didn't know what else to say, so I asked if I could pray for him again.

His countenance softened. This time, tears trickled down his face as I prayed.

Markus stopped crying after several minutes. "You're right. Suicide is not the answer." He seemed to notice the messy house for the first time. "Wow, now what should we do?"

I followed his gaze. "For starters, let's clean up."

After helping Markus, exhaustion hit, so I headed home to bed. Two hours later, a frantic knock at the back door jolted me awake a second time. The clock read 2:00 in the morning. I peered into Twany's face and repeated the desperate prayer that had become my lifeline, "Honey, pray."

Markus stood at the door again. He stormed inside and immediately closed the door behind him. A clean shirt replaced the one stained in blood.

"Can I sleep in your basement?" he asked through ragged breaths. Dark pupils darted back and forth in panic.

Shocked again by his request, I could only think about what Jesus would do. I escorted him to the basement door and returned to my wife to tell her about our house guest.

"Are you crazy?" She glared at me. "He could kill us!"

After further discussion and much prayer, we decided to trust God to protect us.

Within moments, Markus yelled something unintelligible from the basement. It took me a minute to understand he wanted me to talk to people standing outside.

KNIVES AND GUNS

I opened the front door, and my eyes bugged out. A large crowd surrounded my house. Police lights flashed while bright emergency lights flooded the neighborhood.

I blinked, completely dumbfounded. All this activity was happening right outside my home, and I was totally clueless.

Noticing my presence, the police shined their flashlights directly on me. "What do you want?"

I cleared my throat. "The person you want is in our basement. He'll come out soon."

A murmur rose through the crowd as the police prepared for a confrontation. Apparently Markus and his live-in girlfriend had gotten into a fight, so she'd shown up with several friends wielding knives and guns. When Markus saw the weapons, he'd jumped out of the bedroom window and headed for our back door.

Markus stepped outside with a show of brashness that overshadowed the broken man ready to commit suicide a few hours earlier. He swore at his girlfriend, and she shot back with a slew of profanity. The two went back and forth until the police broke up the argument.

An officer approached, agitating Markus further. He shoved the policeman and spit in his face. Shame followed my shock. I'd never seen anyone act with such disrespect toward the police.

"You're headed to jail." Another officer jumped in and cuffed my neighbor. His partner pushed Markus into the squad car.

"Party's over," the first policeman shouted. "Break it up, folks."

The crowd dispersed as the excitement ended. I stood there in my flannel pajamas shell-shocked at the bizarre chain of events.

The next morning after minimal sleep, the phone rang. Markus could get out of jail if he spent house arrest with me while the police finished their investigation.

Twany and I had our reservations, but again, I wondered what Jesus would do. If Markus would commit to daily Bible study, prayer and healthy boundaries with his girlfriend, I would agree to the arrangement. Within a few hours, the police brought our neighbor, a bracelet monitor fastened to his ankle.

Imagine five little kids, Twany, me, and our drug-dealing neighbor living together in one small house. Only God could help us adjust as we studied the Bible together.

The neighborhood took notice. No one could deny the change happening in Markus. Despite my naivety and uncertainty, God's unconditional love flowed through me and my family in simple ways and brought radical change.

A KNOCK ON THE FRONT DOOR, AGAIN

A week later, another knock at the front door made me leap from bed. A small wiry young man who lived across the street stood in front of me with tears in his eyes.

"A few minutes ago, I held a shotgun to my head." His voice caught with emotion. "When I started to pull the trigger, an unknown voice told me to go to the man across the street."

The young man searched my face. "The voice said to talk to you because you know God."

I invited him inside.

"I've seen the change in the guy living in your basement. I want the same thing for my life."

Jake shared how he'd run from home after his father died. Now age 20, he'd survived on the streets for 6 years. Living with his girlfriend and her sister was a hotbed of drugs, prostitution and dysfunction.

Jake wanted to know about Jesus, so I explained how God's son took our punishment when He died on the cross. Jake wanted to surrender his life to Jesus, so we prayed. When Markus moved out a few days later because the police didn't press charges, Jake asked if he could live with us.

"I want to do things right with my girlfriend," Jake explained. "Like God says in the Bible."

What could I say?

Jake moved into the makeshift bedroom in our basement made private by curtains strung across the low ceiling. As I mentored him over the course of the next year, God worked mightily in his life and grounded us in the community of north Omaha.

My heart ignited like never before on that bloody Saturday night when Markus knocked on my door. I was in unfamiliar territory—completely undone—and God had my full attention and affection.

I told Markus that God had a plan for his life, but if I was truthful, I didn't know God's plans for my own days on earth. An honest look at death forced me to think about my present and my future. Even though I'd never sunk to such hopelessness, I didn't have a clear purpose.

As I wrestled with my own mortality, I was no longer content with my own sense of purposelessness. I couldn't sit back and wait for some blueprint to simply fall into my lap. I had to do something. I determined to figure out what God wanted with my life.

In the book of Ephesians, Paul wrote that he didn't want to live thoughtlessly. He wanted to do whatever the Lord asked him to do. Discovering my unique purpose was suddenly a matter of life and death to those around me. God's plan was more than personal; His plan had purpose, a purpose I was desperate to discover.

I WASN'T GOD'S #1 CHOICE

Many times since moving to the inner city, I'd been tempted to return to a safer place of comfort and convenience, but now, I knew I couldn't leave. God wanted me to love my neighbor. He rescued Markus in spite of my inabilities. *But what if I hadn't obeyed the prompting of the Holy Spirit? What if I didn't understand God's purpose for me to love my neighbors?*

I'm sure I was God's last choice to lead an inner city mission. In fact, I probably didn't even make the top ten list. I was afraid, completely unfamiliar with my new surroundings and definitely way over my head. *How could a naïve white guy from rural Iowa be used to make a difference?*

But as long as Jesus gave me time on earth, I wanted to give Him my affection. So I said "yes" to Jesus and became His #1 choice. This affection ignited a passion that compelled me to fully surrender to His plans for my life and to experience a new depth of love for people.

Life-transforming experiences and life-altering environments await us if we simply commit ourselves to intentional involvement in our city.

Jesus said to "love your neighbor," so that's what we would do. North Omaha was exactly where God wanted my family and me.

5

MURDER NEXT DOOR

TRAGEDY, TRAUMA AND HORROR

Twany and I founded ABIDE in north Omaha in April 1989 with the mission to get people out of the seats and into the streets in order to make a difference in our city. Our original focus was threefold: leadership, missions, and unity. I began leading work teams from my church in the suburbs to help churches in the inner city. I consulted with leaders and pastors, including many in north Omaha, to embrace a vision for missions.

God continued to grab my affection through my daily experiences. My heart especially broke for the children. Everyday violence took a huge toll, robbing kids of innocence and producing emotional scars similar to those experienced by soldiers in battle. In an effort to wrap my head around the horror, I read what several children shared. Their firsthand experiences tore me up inside:

- "I saw my mother stab my father with a knife and kill him. She was put in jail; he was dead. I had no one. I see a knife in my dreams every night."
- "They shoot somebody every day. I go in and get under the bed and come out after the shooting stops."

- "It's like the violence is coming down a little closer. We don't come outside a lot now."

- "My daddy got knifed when he got out of jail, and my uncle got shot in a fight. There was a bucket of his blood. I had two aunties killed and one of them was pushed off the freeway and there were maggots on her."

- "They killed my dad as I watched, and I stayed with the body for a very long time, and all the time the killers threatened to kill me, too."

The weight slowly built over the years until I began to question if I misunderstood God's purpose for my life.

MURDER

In March of 1993, almost exactly four years after starting ABIDE, I turned onto our street an hour before midnight. Flashing police lights made my heart race. Yellow crime tape marked off the house next to ours. A crowd of people blocked my path.

"Let's get the kids settled inside, and I'll find out what happened," I told Twany as I inched into our driveway, which was partially blocked due to the investigation.

Shadows darkened the faces around me as I made my way through the throng of people. An ominous feeling made the hair on my neck prickle.

"What happened?" My voice wavered when I saw the swollen eyes of a neighbor woman I recognized.

She broke down. "Chloe and Carissa were murdered."

"What?" I stammered, sure I'd wake up from this nightmare. Chloe and Care Bear were friends of my girls, Kiesha and Coco. They practically lived at our home and regularly attended Bible club with us.

"They found Chloe in the basement." She sobbed. "Carissa's body was left in the abandoned garage in the alley behind your house. Both were shot in the head."

My legs buckled underneath me. The horror made me want to hurl. A dozen memories surfaced. I could hear the girls sing along with my kids as I learned to play the guitar. My lack of talent didn't stop our fun. This couldn't be happening. Chloe and Care Bear couldn't be gone.

The next few hours passed in a blur of surreal conversations with police and reporters. When I finally retreated to my home in the early hours of the morning, flashlights bobbed outside my windows from the continued investigation.

The tears came when I thought about the small bodies carried out on stretchers. My own children slept soundly in their beds, unaware of the ghastly murder of their friends and the unknown suspect still at large.

I called a close friend and anguished over what to do. Family and friends had expressed their concern about our safety before. Now they would beg us to leave the inner city and return to the suburbs and the lucrative field of engineering.

I couldn't argue. My own doubts surfaced. The staggering problems of crime and gang violence overwhelmed me. I'd had one car stolen and another ruined when gang initiates put sugar in the engine. *Was our work in the inner city worth the cost of putting my family in danger? Could we really make a difference in lives? Was it time to quit?*

THE MOST DANGEROUS PLACE TO LIVE

In the quiet before dawn, I sensed God begin to speak. In the midst of my doubt, fear and confusion, I heard Him engage me in a series of questions.

Ron, remember the neighbor woman across the street? The one who looks 60 even though she's 28?

I thought about the young woman with the vacant expression. Hollow eyes met mine whenever I tried to make conversation. Drugs and prostitution had robbed her of her youth.

Can she leave this community?

"Well, no, Lord, she can't."

What about your neighbor who comes knocking on your door asking for his next fix? He's been addicted to drugs for so long, his mind is virtually gone.

I exhaled. This man could barely string together a coherent thought.

Ron, can he leave this community?

"No." I shook my head, knowing poverty, addiction, and circumstances trapped him.

Ron, how about the little girl across the street? You know she's been molested at least three times. You tried to get the police involved, but they said there wasn't enough evidence.

My heart ached at the thought of the sweet 8-year-old trapped in the house of her abuse. The injustice made me want to scream.

Can this abused little girl leave this community?

For the third time, my answer was negative.

I felt God look straight into my eyes. *Then, Ron, neither can you.*

God's heartbeat intersected mine. On that day, He fully grabbed my affection. I resolved to stay in north Omaha, knowing life wouldn't be easy. As God reminded me, the most dangerous place to live wasn't the inner city, but rather outside the center of His will.

TWO SMALL CASKETS

Explaining the murder to our children the next day left me an emotional wreck. Any moment I expected to see Chloe and Carissa appear at our door asking to play. They had planned to attend Bible Club Olympics with my daughters that morning.

A single tear rolled down Coco's face when I told her that Care Bear and Chloe were up in heaven with Jesus. She and Kiesha struggled to understand, and I wanted to spare them details about the murder.

"I love you." I hugged them close, grateful for their lives and saddened once again for the tragic loss of their friends.

I didn't know how I'd make it through the funeral. Pain knifed my heart when I saw the lifeless bodies inside the two small caskets. Freckles smattered Carissa's face while Chloe's lips turned into the hint of a smile. Red roses lined their sides and notes written in crayons rested on their blue print dresses. Their mother wanted me to speak, yet what could I say?

I knew the girls' bodies were suitcases housing both spirit and soul, but seeing the finality of life weighted me. Emotions overwhelmed me.

Ron? I heard God call my name. *Could you give your life to this community so other kids won't have their lives cut short by violence?*

God was asking for a new depth of surrender. I looked at my kids sitting in the church pew, their heads descending like steps in a staircase, and I knew my answer.

Being in the center of God's will is never easy, but it's always fulfilling. For most of my life, I didn't get around broken people enough to awaken a passion beyond my own children and family. Living in the inner city made me face life's ugly realities every single day. I'd invited Jesus into my heart as a new believer, but now Jesus was inviting me into His. What broke the heart of God now broke mine.

Seeing the lifeless bodies of my neighbor girls angered me. The injustice stirred up holy discontent, which awakened deep passion. My heart ached over the emptiness and injustice around me.

I couldn't return to life back in Velveetaville like nothing had happened. Too many kids like Carissa and Chloe would lose their lives to senseless tragedy. I had no choice. I would give my life for my neighbors.

6

THE HEART OF CHRISTIANITY

THE LIFESTYLE OF A CHRIST FOLLOWER

I'd never thought of Christianity in terms of a *lifestyle* until God grabbed my affection. Before He gave me His love for others, I thought Christianity was more about having deep convictions and beliefs.

I calculated my growth as a Christian by the amount of time spent studying scripture. But the more churched I got, the more comfortable I grew. My head knowledge rarely translated to heart knowledge. The more religious I got, the less relational I became and the less I needed God. Slowly I began to realize my version of Christianity was incomplete.

I lived with an overwhelming emphasis on having the right set of beliefs in order to truly be a Christian. My academic pursuits and chemical engineering background tilted me toward knowledge and understanding. I considered myself a risk-taker when I defended my beliefs and debated right and wrong, but I discovered God's definition looked different. Risk-taking faith was a relational *lifestyle* that attracted people into the arms of Jesus. That type of faith didn't exist in me.

Brutally honest. But true.

My calendar and my checkbook showed my values. I lived like my non-Christian neighbors. Same house, same cars, same vacations, same purchases. The only exception was my church attendance and Bible study classes. While I could affirm the tenets of my faith, my neighbors couldn't confirm Jesus had radically changed my life.

JUST LIKE BREATHING, CHRISTIANITY HAS TWO PARTS

I felt smothered by Velveetaville until God brought me to the inner city. Just like physical life is sustained when we inhale and exhale, the same is true of Christianity. Ezekiel 37:10 says, "Breath entered them (and) they came to life." (NIV) Until God shook my world, I didn't realize Christianity involved two parts: a personal relationship and a purposeful relationship with Jesus.

My suffocation came because only one dimension of my faith was functioning. I received through my personal relationship with Jesus, but I didn't share my life with others through a purposeful relationship with Jesus. Both were essential to my spiritual life. On the one hand, I needed to *tend* to my relationship with Jesus while on the other hand, I needed to *extend* my life to others.

As God kindled my affection for my neighbors, the brokenness I saw transformed me and stirred me to action. Similar to Jeremiah 20:9, passion ignited "a burning fire shut up in my bones," propelling me with a force I couldn't contain. (NKJV)

My faith moved from personal to practical. When God broke my heart and grabbed my attention, He moved me beyond my beliefs to a transformed lifestyle.

Living in the inner city challenged me to back up my beliefs through my everyday actions. Allowing Jesus to invite me into his heart moved me to a place of vulnerability and availability that added incredible fulfillment and purpose to my life. Truths that I understood about Christianity were increasingly being shaped into something even more powerful than what I had previously known. This inward change manifested in outward change.

LIVE TO CARE, DIE TO FEAR

When God ignited my affection, he gave me a new love for my neighbors. I no longer stood on the sidelines pointing out problems in the inner city. I saw the faces of my neighbors. Brokenness and hopelessness tore my heart.

The more I lived to care, the more I died to fear. Friends and family worried about our safety, but love took over and fear no longer bound me. I had a choice—either focus on the enemy and look for danger around every corner or look to my savior and trust Jesus to protect my family and me. God fully had my affection, and His love overtook my fears and filled me with a deep compassion for my neighbors.

In the book of Luke, Jesus said the second greatest commandment after loving God was loving our neighbor. An expert in the law tried to find a loophole, a way out, so he questioned Jesus, asking, "Who is my neighbor?"

Jesus answered by sharing the story of a Samaritan, a priest and a Levite who came upon a man who had been beaten and robbed. The priest didn't want to get involved while the Levite avoided the man and kept his distance. Both religious leaders remained apathetic to the hurting man.

Compassion, however, moved the Samaritan. Self-focus didn't blind him to the need of others. He postponed his plans rather than let busyness distract him. The Samaritan accepted the cost and sacrificed what he had to help his neighbor. Jesus told the expert in the law to show the same mercy.

If crime and violence darkened the world, the church—me—needed to shine brighter. If I refused to get involved in the inner city and chose apathy and avoidance, darkness would prevail.

Darkness is the absence of light, so there's no hope unless light shows up. Darkness never invades light. Light always dispels darkness.

My neighbors needed the hope residing in me. The darkness around me would be filled with brightness if I, as light, showed up. Showing up meant getting out of my seat and into the street.

Living Intentionally Versus Accidentally

I yearned for my life to matter, yet too often I found myself going through the motions and missing out on abundant life. I lived life accidentally rather than intentionally. No matter how hard I studied the Bible, my life didn't look any different from everyone around me.

I imagined standing before God and explaining why my life didn't matter. I wasn't an accident, yet it was so easy to live accidentally. I needed to surrender to His plan. Anything less would be a life filled with regret and unfulfilled dreams.

Living in the inner city showed me the first key to living intentionally was recognizing God's heart for the broken. He continually used people and circumstances to pull me from the temporal and refocus on the eternal. Through this ongoing process, God brought clarity to my life and propelled me to live differently—full of His presence, passion, purpose and power.

The second key was allowing discomfort and interruptions to invade my life, no matter how inconvenient or how irksome. Coming from the suburbs with its comfortable predictability, I sometimes wrestled with God's interruptions— especially when they came after midnight.

INTERRUPTIONS

Frankie showed up at my house at 2 a.m., stoned and wasted, a case of beer under his arm.

"She's sleeping with someone," Frankie's words slurred together.

I wiped the sleep from my eyes and looked at the defeated man on my doorstep. The old Ron wanted to send him home and curl back next to my wife. *What could I do at this hour anyway?* I'd been helping Frankie and his wife for several weeks. *Couldn't we just talk the next day after a night of sleep?*

Frankie shifted his weight and stumbled, crumbling my own internal tension. I couldn't send him back home. Frankie would be a target wandering the streets at this hour.

"Come in." I helped steady him. "You can have my son's bed."

The next morning, Frankie and I talked. While I couldn't solve his marriage issues, I told him about the One who could. Despite the night's interruption, I was grateful Frankie saw hope in me and wanted the same for his life.

Interruptions can feel like derailments at the time, but God always has something bigger in mind. Scripture is full of accounts where God brought revelation to people, and their intentional follow-through resulted in eternal change. He interrupted Moses' life and saved Israel. God interrupted Queen Esther's life and saved the Jewish people. God interrupted Paul's life and propelled the gospel beyond the Jewish nation. Love for people is always at the root of God's interruptions.

Love costs, but when God grabs our affection, the cost diminishes in light of eternity. Like the parable in the Bible of the merchant who sold everything to buy a pearl of great value, I was willing to pay the price. God grabbed my affection for my neighbors in the inner city and taught me:

- I wouldn't die until Jesus was finished with me.
- God had a plan for my life.
- God is comfortable when I'm uncomfortable.
- Living outside the center of God's will is the most dangerous place to live—not the inner city.
- When I lived to care, I died to fear.
- Living intentionally meant letting God interrupt my life.

The more God grabbed my affection, the more He called me to action. He wanted to shine through me, so His light could dispel the darkness around me.

WHEN GOD CALLS US TO ACTION

7

LIVING
DANGEROUSLY

SAFETY OR IMPACT?

Early Christians put obedience to Christ first. Risking their lives for the gospel was normal. Advancing Christ's kingdom overshadowed all other priorities. Even if many people couldn't understand this call to action, this same passion consumed me after the murder of our neighbor girls. Twany and I fielded numerous questions, especially concerns about the safety of our children. *Weren't they in danger?*

Reality painted a grim picture. In many ways, life was riskier in the inner city than in the suburbs. This truth was forefront in conversations with our children as we continually reminded and reassured them that God was in control. While living outside the center of God's will was the most dangerous place to live, living inside the center of His will didn't guarantee our safety either. Rather, the temporary danger we faced couldn't compare to the eternal safety and significance of living for Christ.

Even before the double homicide unsettled our world, God showed me that my children were not my own. On a quiet evening while Twany had plans, I cleaned the garage, and the kids played outside.

"Daddy, Daddy!" Nekiesha ran up to me frantically. "The neighbors have guns."

103

I rushed to gather my kids together and looked across the street. Several teenage boys stuffed guns under the front seat of an old sedan in preparation for their evening festivities.

I tightened my grip on my kids and breathed a frightened prayer. "I will go anywhere, God, but I can't risk the lives of my children."

Before the words left my lips, I heard Him ask, *Whose children?*

Countless sermons on parenting suddenly took on new significance. My children were God's children, and I was simply His steward. My job was to raise His children for His honor and purposes. But my heart said otherwise. *Did my lifestyle reflect my beliefs? Could I truly trust God to care for my children in a dangerous place?*

In a deeper level of awareness and submission, I surrendered my control and ownership of my children to the Lord.

RAISING RADICAL WORLD-CHANGING CHILDREN

Alarming statistics show a high percentage of all children raised in church no longer attend church or plan to return. Ask why, and young people express knowing a lot about the Christian faith, but little about living a Christian lifestyle.

Unless our kids see us feeding the homeless or working with the needy, they don't see faith in action. Attending church, participating in Bible studies, and going to Christ-centered summer camp falls short. We need to get out of the seats and into the streets if we want to prepare our kids to live fully committed lives to Christ. Otherwise young people feel cheated because what they see modeled at home doesn't align with what they hear year after year sitting in church.

Like all parents, Twany and I possess the natural instinct to protect our kids. But life in the inner city taught us we did more harm if we failed to prepare our kids. The farm effect has shown that being exposed to allergens early in life helps a child's immune system. In other words, exposing our kids to dirt actually protects them. The same is true in life. Isolating our kids from bumps, bruises and germs doesn't prepare them to live in a world where they're going to fall down and get sick.

My wife and I soon realized parenting wasn't simply about protecting our kids from the bad things in our world. As Christians, the two of us have been given a serious responsibility to raise children who influence the world for Jesus. Our children need to be empowered to advance

Christ's kingdom in the middle of the mess. Exposing our kids to poverty, pain and brokenness births compassion and shapes their hearts more than any Bible study ever could.

Risk is at the heart of the faith journey—both for children and adults. As parents, Twany and I have a responsibility to model faith in a troubled world. The life we are called to live includes our children. Discipleship happens in the context of family life. They need to see us take risks for Christ and experience risk themselves. When we overprotect our children, we don't allow them to take healthy steps of faith and become authentic Christians.

Not only do Twany and I involve our children locally in the inner city, we want them to connect globally in impoverished countries. Our passion is for our children to embrace the whole world. Before graduation, we require each one to visit another country and serve on a mission venture. We model the life we want them to follow.

Twany and I are far from perfect parents, but we have intentionally committed to raising our 14 children to be Christians who don't sit on the sidelines. They don't know the Bible better than their peers. They may skip a morning devotion or forget to pray, but they've witnessed evil and the traps of addictions, and they've seen the hope Jesus offers.

As Christian parents, we need to strap on our seatbelts for a difficult ride. We are not called to raise good little boys and girls who will have a nice career and a comfortable life. Rather we stand at the front lines of the battle, releasing a radical generation of world-changers who will get out of the seats and into the streets and accept God's call to action.

BELIEFS ARE MORE FORMED THAN INFORMED

People ask me all the time how Twany and I balance raising a healthy family while serving in the inner city. The question itself is imbalanced, implying conflict between health and involvement in Christ's mission. According to the culture's definition, our family isn't balanced at all. And that's a good thing. We are completely committed to the cause of Christ and pursuing God's rhythm for our lives. If that means our kids don't play every sport or join every school club, that's okay.

We get on our knees together, and we roll up our sleeves together. Ministry time and family time go hand in hand as we integrate our Christian values everywhere we go. Ministry isn't just for professionals and adults. As young as sixth grade, we take our children to leadership conferences for their development. Watching our kids display their unique gifts during neighborhood

107

connections, family interactions, school activities, church ministry, and short-term mission trips is powerful.

As Christ's followers, we exist as ambassadors and aliens on this earth in order to fully give ourselves to transforming a broken world. God's mission in the world is our top priority. Nothing short of living out this charge will do.

Matthew 7:24 challenges us to be purposeful by putting scripture into practice. Biblical knowledge learned in a safe environment like a church sanctuary doesn't reach the heart and affect behavior without an experience to practice what we believe. Knowledge can't take root and produce fruit unless we are placed in environments that reinforce what we learned.

Our experiences shape the people we become. Two foreign mission trips showed me how beliefs—which ultimately drive behavior—are more formed by experiences than informed by teaching. The first was a trip to serve street children in Africa. Mealtime chaos was a shock until the orphanage staff explained why the kids acted so crudely. Because of the uncertainty of going without food, boys and girls horded leftovers in their pockets and frantically shoveled food into their mouths to prevent theft. Using dinnerware was an anomaly.

Teaching etiquette to these street kids was a huge undertaking for the orphanage staff. Informing them of the need to use dinnerware didn't change their behavior. Hunger, abuse and harsh living conditions had shaped their beliefs for so long, they needed to form a new set of beliefs. The kids had to believe they would be fed consistently or their behavior wouldn't change.

A second mission trip to China confronted me with the same reality that beliefs were more formed than informed. For years, I'd heard of killings and imprisonment of Christians in China. I visited the country to help teach Chinese pastors and leaders about the Bible, but they taught me far more.

Early in the morning my hosts drove me to a high-rise corporate building like many of the other sky-scrapers surrounding us. Once we arrived, my hosts gave me the following instructions:

Say nothing.
Cover your head with your hood.
Bow.
Follow the person in front of you.
Walk quickly.
Do not look around.

The hair on my flesh rose to attention. I wasn't some secret agent in an action movie. Anything could happen, and the unknown frightened me. I'd only begun to understand what reality meant to Chinese Christians.

Inside the corporate building, we took the stairs rather than the elevator. We walked quickly, exiting the fourth floor out of breath. The degree of precautionary measures surprised me. We took the elevator up several flights of floors and repeated the process. Rush up the stairs. Exit. Take the elevator. Repeat.

Once at our destination, and somewhat exhausted from the stairway climb, I peeked out from under my hoodie. Several people stood inside the room, their posture quiet, yet welcoming. As we walked down the hallway, the smiles and conversation bore evidence that we'd arrived on a "safe" floor.

Just as I started to let my guard down, further precautions were taken. My hosts rushed me into a soundproof room similar to a recording studio built inside a larger room for the protection of Christians against an unfriendly Chinese government. Two doors quickly shut upon my entrance. Security and privacy were of utmost importance.

This was not my "safe" Christianity back in the suburbs of Velveetaville. Faith had formed these Chinese Christians. They lived out their beliefs in a lifestyle formed by their risk-taking faith. Living in constant threat drove Chinese Christians to worship in secret—something I never considered because my own belief system was shaped by a culture that respected freedom of religion. My own vulnerability as a believer was minimal at best. *Would I risk prison for my faith? A beating? Death?*

Like the different cultures I'd experienced on these two mission trips, life in the inner city came with a new set of unwritten rules. Poverty and injustice had shaped the beliefs of my neighbors. Bible knowledge wasn't enough to change their behavior. My neighbors needed new experiences with authentic Christians and a real God.

The Bible illustrates this formation process in Jeremiah 18 using the idea of clay being formed on the potter's wheel. God uses the pressures of life—hardships, experiences, interactions, and relationships—to form each of us into the unique pot He sees for the purpose He intends. Water, His word, is necessary to smooth out our rough texture while His fingers imprint His love into our lives.

We are all in process. Positioning ourselves—and our children—in unfamiliar, uncomfortable or culturally different environments exposes deeply imbedded beliefs and behavior which don't parallel scripture. God loves us too much to let us stagnate, so these *exposure* moments become opportunities to realign our lives with His plan. We experience Jesus in the brokenness of the world as we encounter real people who are experiencing real challenges.

EVERYTHING WAS STOLEN

My children demonstrated proof of God's formation process one morning as our family drove along our street toward home. Two little neighbor girls giggled as they shared a single pair of roller skates. One wore a skate on her right foot while the other girl wore the other skate on her left foot. They held hands and rolled down the sidewalk, falling more than staying upright. Other children smiled and laughed as they rode bikes and played with more toys. The sight of their happiness was contagious. To see this sweet innocence in the inner city brought joy to my heart.

"Hey those are my roller skates," one of my daughters suddenly exclaimed from the back seat.

"And that's my bicycle," her brother echoed. "We should get it back."

Realization swept over the van. All the toys, bikes and skates belonged to my children. A few weeks earlier someone had broken into our garage and stolen most of its contents.

I faced my children with a smile. "We're going to let these kids keep everything because they're having so much fun. Besides, look how much joy it brings us to give them our toys."

Not one of my kids whined. Rather, their quick acceptance and resilience bore evidence to how God was shaping them through life in the inner city. Matthew 6:20 wasn't simply a scripture verse the kids memorized in Sunday school. "Store up for yourselves treasures in heaven, where moths and vermin do not destroy, and where thieves do not break in and steal." (NIV) Experiences like this formed—not just informed—my children to accept God's call to action and live out the principles in His word.

That's the substance of real heart change.

CHAPTER

8

PASSION FOR THE LOST

MAPS AND BULLETS,
AN URGENT REMINDER

I have a crime map of a two-mile radius of my inner city neighborhood that the police gave me. Our team also gathered data to build a murder map that hangs at ABIDE headquarters. Red pins cover the map, bleeding primarily over north Omaha. Each pin represents an individual murdered in our city since 1991. Close to two-thirds of the homicides in Omaha occur in this murder zone. Every time we update the map with another red pin, my heart hurts for the loss of life.

Though most of us don't decorate our homes with such graphic pictures, Christ followers need visual reminders of our call to action. We need to be angry enough at violence to act and passionate enough to give our lives. This passion fills us with urgency for people headed to an eternity separated from Christ.

I carry five bullets in my pocket to keep this urgency at the forefront of my mind. My children found four of them in our yard while the fifth was found in the house next door. When I wrap my fingers around the cold metal, I can't forget the murder of our two neighbor girls, as well as the many others represented by the pins on the murder map. Unless I'm traveling by plane, I carry these reminders with me every day. Before I even pocket the bullets, I whisper a prayer for my neighbors and my city.

Both the murder map and the bullets give me a sense of urgency to live life with purpose. These visual reminders of the pain and suffering in my city break my heart. If I'm part of the solution, I'm pressed to live my life in such a way as to impact as many people as possible. My life is too important to waste on trivial and temporary things. Passion drives me to fulfill my eternal purpose and call to action.

Seeing these visuals on display sparked a vision from God that one day people from all over the world would fly into Omaha because there would be no inner city. Omaha would be a city without crime and violence. Employment and education would soar, and every child would live in a loving home with a committed father and mother to nurture them.

Maps and bullets are my visual reminders of the urgency I need to live my life. Every gunshot and murder reminds me there is more work to be done as echoed in Ephesians 5:15-16. "Be very careful, then, how you live . . . making the most of every opportunity, because the days are evil." (NIV)

WE NEED THE POOR

I once asked a businessman what he could provide for my inner city community. His quick answer—jobs, money, training and education— would definitely benefit my neighbors. However, when I asked him what my community could provide for him, he stammered, finally answering, "Nothing."

The sting of his words hurt because I would've said the same thing before brokenness broke me.

The poor have something powerful to teach us about life. The absence of material possessions simplifies life, allowing us to focus on what is most important—relationships. My abundance of "stuff" gave me a sense of superiority so that I looked down on people that didn't achieve the same level of "success." When relationships became central to my life, I found a richness and fulfillment I hadn't experienced while chasing after the American dream.

Positioning ourselves in relationships with the poor humbles us and shows us the dignity of all God's people and their valuable contribution to the kingdom.

From my couch in Velveetaville, I turned on the evening news and took sides. Instead of seeing the underlying issues of poverty and crime, I simplified the problems to good versus evil. I saw gang members as the epitome of evil, taking lives and causing havoc. But when I got next to brokenness, I saw kids like my own needing love, validation and security. Those "evil" gang members were real people created in God's image with incredible potential to make contributions to His kingdom—contributions I couldn't make.

Ephesians 6:12 says, "For our struggle is not against flesh and blood, but against the rulers, against the authorities, against the powers of this dark world and against the spiritual forces of evil in the heavenly realms." (NIV) This narrative plays out from super heroes and villains to favorite sports teams and their arch-rivals. We are quick to judge what is good or evil. The Bible makes it very clear that there is ultimate evil in the world, but it's not people.

The battle is for lives, and the real enemy wants to steal, kill and destroy. But Jesus came to give abundant life. (John 10:10 NKJV) Most of these gangsters were kids who were one bad choice from ending up on the evening news. Like me, they were lost and in need of a savior. *Was I willing to humble myself, get involved, and lay down my life so others could come to know Jesus?*

BROKENNESS ENGAGES THE CHURCH TO LOVE

My plea for pastors is to reconnect the church to the city. This call to action goes beyond churches simply giving money to foreign missions and local nonprofit ministries. Giving money without regularly giving our time to areas of need within our communities wedges distance between the churched and unchurched. Christians need to personally connect with brokenness to connect with God's heart. When we are broken over what breaks God's heart, passion compels us to action.

My life in Velveetaville lacked passion. Lost people were dying around me, but I wasn't moved enough to act. The amount of money I made allowed me to distance myself from the spiritually broken. God took the physical brokenness of the inner city to ignite spiritual passion in me. My passion for the hurting in my city correlated with the distance between me and the broken. The greater the distance, the less passion I had. The smaller the distance, the more passion compelled me to action.

Love engages the church with the brokenness in our city. Serving the broken on a consistent basis gets the church out of the seats and into the streets where Christians can practice living out the truths of the Bible. As leaders, we have to create environments where Christ followers can learn to share their faith as they serve the unchurched and grow in a purposeful relationship with Jesus.

Jesus had many names—Messiah, Deliverer, Good Shepherd, Holy One, King of Kings—but perhaps the most interesting name is "friend of sinners." (Matthew 11:19 NIV) His relationships and proximity to sinners made the religious uncomfortable, but passion for lost people consumed Jesus.

Being next to brokenness increases our reliance on God and awakens our faith to new levels. Revelation 3 warns about lukewarm Christianity a.k.a. Velveetaville Christianity. Brokenness heats up our faith until it boils with passion for the lost and hurting in our city. Staying near the heat source—brokenness—is paramount as Christians.

We will never transform the brokenness of our city until the brokenness of our city transforms us. God stirs our compassion when we face poverty, pain and difficulties. If I commit myself to serving the broken and the needy, God will use me to make an impact in the world.

When I coached soccer at a YMCA in the inner city, Twany and I befriended a single mom of five young kids. One night she called to ask me to rescue her boyfriend from a local bar. The very thought made me recoil inside. I had left the bar scene ten years earlier. Nothing good could come from hanging out at a north Omaha bar after midnight.

I wanted to find an excuse, but I couldn't let this single mom down after she reached out to me. I got out of bed and drove through the dark streets, praying God would keep me safe.

Geno sat alone on a bar stool aimlessly holding his drink. When I took the seat next to him, recognition sparked in his bloodshot eyes. "You here to get me?"

I nodded, and he stumbled alongside me toward my van. "My life's a mess," he slobbered through our conversation. Compassion filled me as he told me parts of his story.

"There is hope," I finally interjected when he quieted. Dull eyes searched mine, wanting to believe my words. "His name is Jesus."

Not only did Geno become a Christian in the early hours of that morning, he temporarily moved into a property we'd acquired and landed a job. He and his girlfriend got married, and I began discipling them.

Going to an inner city bar at midnight was far from comfortable, but when adversity is connected to God's calling, which is bigger than my own desires, accepting the call to action is easier. God wants me to pay attention to tension because adversity always brings opportunity to show love and bring hope to lost and broken people.

TAKE A STEP

Impacting the world for God begins when I take one step. God isn't asking for 100 steps; He's simply asking me to take the next step.

Psalm 37:23 says, "The steps of a good man are ordered by the LORD." (NKJV) Fear can easily paralyze me when I consider the entire journey, but the concept of steps reveals God's heart. His ways are gentle as He leads me one step at a time to fully develop me into maturity.

Christianity is a movement because God is constantly at work changing me to change the world. When I humbly submit to His will for my life, He changes me. Whether I become more loving and caring, or whether I share my faith more actively, these growth moments are a critical part of my Christian life. Each step brings the fullness of God's presence. Incredible potential is realized the more I grow, producing powerful transformation in my life and the lives of those I impact.

Action reflects my passion. When is the last time I invited someone to church? When is the last time I shared my faith story with a nonbeliever?

Every activity in my day brings opportunities. Buying groceries, working out, going to a restaurant all become places to look for the Holy Spirit to move. A simple prayer thanking a server or an invitation to church may be just the next step to bring someone closer to Jesus. Other times, an opportunity opens for me to share my faith in a simple three minute conversation. What did my life look like before Christ? What circumstances led to my desire for change? How am I different with Christ? Gone are the days when I tried to convince people through an argument. No one can debate my experiences with a living God.

Passion is not an option for radical, world-changing Christians called to action. Otherwise I miss out on abundant life and become apathetic, stale and comfortable. I become impotent and no longer touch others, inviting them into an amazing relationship with Jesus Christ.

A few years ago, I began starting the day with this prayer. "Lord, today I give you permission to change me. And then Lord, use me to change the world."

Watch out world. God answers radical prayers, and He uses changed people to change people.

CHAPTER

9

TIME TO ACT

CHURCHES AND
THE MURDER ZONE

Living in the inner city came with an abundance of challenges. The constant needs overwhelmed me as the days stretched into years. Founding one nonprofit organization wasn't enough. Too many people needed help. In addition to ABIDE, I helped start—indirectly or directly—two dozen nonprofits and spent considerable time and energy on programs. However, after more than 15 years of nonprofit work through ABIDE and these other inner city organizations, little changed. Burnout and lack of progress left me hopeless and threatened to render me useless.

Extremely disheartening was the lack of true disciple-making that occurred in my programmatic approach. Even though all the nonprofits were faith-based, kids didn't connect to churches and weren't growing in their faith. The programs played a role in educating and employing young people, but fell short in developing authentic Christ-centered disciples. Many of the same kids I *helped* landed in a casket or a prison cell because of lack of real behavioral change. Despite years of work, local and national news articles reported crime, violence, and poverty in the inner city was actually getting worse. These articles, along with frequent visits to funerals and prisons, burdened my heart.

One newspaper article was particularly sobering because 31 shootings happened within the time span of a single summer month. As I stared at the pictured faces and saw the listed addresses— houses to my left and to my right—I felt God jolt my attention once again. My neighbors were dying around me despite all my years living and working in the inner city. I couldn't keep doing things the same way and expect different results.

Jesus came to save the lost and build the church. He prayed that the kingdom of heaven would come on earth. As one of Christ's followers, my purpose was to build Christ's kingdom, to keep His church central to everything I do, to live with a passion that drives me to share the gospel, and to fulfill the mandate to make disciples. True biblical discipleship, embedded in the activity of the local church family, would transform broken lives.

I was one of many Christians who worshipped inside the four walls of a church building while children were being murdered just outside of the doors, and none of us took action. No wonder the unchurched couldn't believe Christianity really mattered. Churches weren't making things better.

Compounding this indictment of ineffectiveness, over 100 of Omaha's 600 churches were located in the murder zone. Sadly, more churches were concentrated in this zone than anywhere else in the city. Cynics who saw the murder map in the office at ABIDE quipped, "If you want an immoral, crime-ridden neighborhood, just plant a church."

Ouch.

DISCONTENTED AND UNSETTLED

My heart became increasingly discontented and unsettled the more God filled me with love for my hurting neighbors. I burned with a desire to see the beauty of God's people transforming the brokenness in our city.

Living in the inner city only fueled this growing disgruntlement. I felt like shouting from the spires of churches across my city to rally my brothers and sisters. *Where is our passion? Have we lost our purpose? Was Christ being formed in us, or did we attend church just to be informed? Why didn't leaders like me channel other Christians within the church to transform our cities?*

Four primary areas of concern kept me on my knees, searching the heart of God for answers.

Lack of passion.

Lack of purpose.

Lack of discipleship.

Lack of leadership.

Our city was dying for hope, and my futile efforts reminded me that something was missing. I knew God called me to action, but once again, I reached the end of myself. I had to change what ABIDE was doing, or we would continue to spin in vain circles.

The church-planting team that would birth Bridge Church joined me in prayer. As we opened our hearts to God, I found myself reciting the familiar words of the Lord's Prayer. "Our Father in heaven, hallowed be your name, your kingdom come, your will be done, on earth as it is in heaven."

I stopped mid-phrase and opened my eyes to stare at the various members of our team. "With all this crime and murder, what does heaven look like in our neighborhood?"

"Cleaner," someone piped up.

"Safer," another voice added.

An idea began to take shape in my mind. "Why don't we start by picking up trash and mowing lawns?"

The concept was simple. Love our neighbors in practical ways by getting out of the seats and cleaning up the streets. With this small beginning, ABIDE refocused our mission and began with a grassroots neighborhood approach.

God moved from getting my attention and grabbing my affection to calling me to action, He wanted me:

- To model what I wanted my kids to follow and raise radical world-changers.
- To *tend* to my personal relationship with Jesus while I *extended* my life to others in a purposeful relationship with Jesus.
- To fuel my passion with visual reminders of brokenness and fill me with urgency for people headed to an eternity separated from Christ.
- To position myself next to brokenness to increase my reliance on God and awaken my faith to new levels.
- To pay attention to tension because adversity brings opportunity to show love and bring hope to lost and broken people.
- To take the first step and actually do something.

Understanding these principles launched ABIDE into a new season of growth and effectiveness.

Section II:
Into the Streets

ABIDE:
ADOPTING
NEIGHBORHOODS

10

LIGHTHOUSES AND NEIGHBORHOOD BEAUTIFICATION

THE BIBLICAL CHURCH

Impassioned and compelled to impact as many people as possible, I started to rethink how the church and the nonprofit could function together in order to make the most difference. God had radically changed me. Now I wanted to help others experience the same change by modeling how the church and nonprofit could collaborate to effectively transform the brokenness in our city.

The strengths of the nonprofit were many. Nonprofits engaged and connected with people far from Christ. Their programmatic approach addressed specific needs that were crucial and important to the growth and development of children and adults. Nonprofits provided houses, addiction recovery, homeless shelters, educational opportunities, and many other worthwhile benefits to society. The nonprofit played a significant role in many lives as an important factor in the equation of success.

Churches, on the other hand, provided a moral compass, driving people to act in kindness, gentleness, and in fairness to one another. Churches cared for the sick and marginalized. Acting as a "womb to tomb" support network, churches strengthened people to fulfill their incredible potential. The church not only helped people express worship to a holy God, the church empowered people to extend God's love to those seeking hope and kept eternal hope alive in hearts, compelling Christians to act in Christ-like fashion.

Merging the existing model of the church and the nonprofit is what the scriptures would call "the church." As followers of Christ, we join Jesus in building his church. The nonprofit must therefore move people into a local church family as a "womb to tomb" lifeline and comprehensive disciple-making team.

When the church and the nonprofit are separated from each other, neither makes the desired impact. The church misses out on opportunities to transform lives in the city if not fully intertwined with the nonprofit while the nonprofit loses the sustainable and comprehensive impact the church offers. Working together, the church and the nonprofit powerfully impact lives both temporarily and eternally.

The vision to impact the inner city became clearer when ABIDE united with Bridge Church. The lessons God had been teaching me helped launch ABIDE into an unparalleled season of growth and effectiveness. My son Josh captured the heart of ABIDE's new focus through the following acronym:

Adopting Neighborhoods
Bridge Churches
Invest in Leaders
Diversity
Engage Partners

PUTTING THE NEIGHBOR BACK IN THE HOOD

As our team continued to dream of a day with no more inner city, ABIDE streamlined our efforts and focused on these five areas in our ongoing effort to impact the north Omaha community. When Jesus said to "love your neighbor," He really meant something. Loving our neighbor was His strategy to change our city.

In Omaha, the inner city could be broken into 700 targeted neighborhoods. Each neighborhood equaled one street with houses across the road from each other. With an average of 25 houses and 4 people living in each house, our target was 100 people per neighborhood. By creating safety and security in neighborhoods—basic needs according to Maslow's Hierarchy of Needs—people in the inner city could reach the higher levels of belonging, confidence and achievement.

NEIGHBORHOOD APPROACH

When ABIDE began its neighborhood approach in 2007, one of the biggest issues facing the north Omaha community was the amount of dilapidated and abandoned properties. With over 3,200 properties considered condemned and more houses with code violations or listed for demolition, the problem seemed daunting. When owners didn't maintain their homes, care for the community diminished and crime flourished. Police call this the "broken window" effect because unmaintained neighborhoods and condemned houses become havens for drugs, gangs and violence. The police told us cleaner neighborhoods were safer neighborhoods.

ABIDE targeted two crime-ridden neighborhoods for its first efforts at cleaning up. Two houses—just blocks apart—quickly became the focus when ABIDE bought the properties in the summer of 2008. With the help of an army of volunteers and the first church partnership, the houses on Fowler and Larimore were gutted and remodeled.

Before the transformation, graffiti covered the walls and drug syringes littered the Fowler house which had been abandoned for 13 years. This house served as a catalyst for change in the neighborhood. With each improvement to the house, one neighbor after another emerged from the surrounding houses. Neighbors began to watch out for each other. The transformation of just one home brought dramatic change to the entire neighborhood. The Larimore house mirrored the same effect.

Picking up trash, mowing empty lots and fixing abandoned properties caused a decrease in crime in these two neighborhoods, and the police took notice. When officers asked the neighbors what happened, they pointed to our home which also housed the ABIDE office.

"We don't know what's going on," the police told me. "But whatever you've been doing is working. Two years ago, this was one of the worst neighborhoods in Omaha. Today, it's one of the best."

As a result, the Lighthouse concept was born. When the Fowler house neared completion, following the example Twany and I set 20 years earlier, a family from ABIDE's partner Bridge Church was recruited to live in the Lighthouse. In addition to becoming an advocate for the neighborhood, the Lighthouse family would build relationships with neighbors through tangible acts of love.

Lighthouses are donated or purchased at a fraction of the cost and then completely renovated. Houses are gutted down to the studs and installed with new plumbing, electrical and HVAC systems. With the support of ABIDE's partners and donors, remodels cost a third to half of the standard cost. The benefits are priceless. Crime drops and neighbors are empowered to change their neighborhoods.

Seven years later, the original house on Fowler is now one of 21 Lighthouses which have been renovated. Nine more Lighthouses are currently being remodeled and 104 neighborhoods have been adopted. Street by street, one home at a time, ABIDE volunteers are transforming neighborhoods by renovating abandoned houses and providing activities for kids and adults in the neighborhoods. Through relationships with Lighthouse families, neighbors connect to ABIDE's community building events, family support programs, and Bridge Church where lives begin to transform.

Volunteers like Jim and Diann learned about ABIDE's housing program through their church in the suburbs of Omaha at a time when they were considering ways to serve in a mission program. Five years and two houses later, Jim and Diann do more than just help with the renovation process. They continue to visit the neighborhoods each month to get to know the neighbors.

As one Lighthouse resident reported, "Being in a Lighthouse has expanded our focus to include serving those in a blighted neighborhood. It's a reminder that we have a responsibility and a stewardship to let people know that when they have Jesus, life can be better."

WHEN THE SPIRITUAL GETS PRACTICAL

Gunshots followed the sound of screeching tires in one of ABIDE's Lighthouse neighborhoods. A car careened down the street, crashing in and out of yards, knocking out two fences, and hitting a tree stump before flipping onto its roof. Blood covered the driver who had been shot.

Two young men who lived near the Lighthouse, immediately ran to the scene of the accident. One was my son Jeremiah's best friend, Bryson. The other was Raymond.

The two frantically called 911 and assisted the driver with his injuries. The police showed up and placed Bryson and Raymond in handcuffs during their investigation. Word spread quickly to the Lighthouse family who knew the teenagers from ABIDE's youth programs. They joined Bryson and Raymond's families at the scene of the crime, praying and comforting them. After four long hours, the police uncovered a drug deal gone wrong and released the young men.

As a result of ABIDE's neighborhood approach and our presence in this situation, we were recognized as a catalyst for change in our community. We were invited to work with the police and the city government to make a difference in north Omaha.

ROSIE

Rosie was a member of one of ABIDE's partner churches, and while she worked among high-risk, low-income families, she had a distrust of the north Omaha community. When her church volunteered at a block party, Rosie drove around the neighborhood with her children to determine how safe she felt before volunteering at the next event. After hearing from her husband how safe and enjoyable the block party had been, she decided to find out more about ABIDE.

Rosie and her husband, Jim, have a multiethnic family. Because their home church was not very ethnically diverse, their children didn't always feel like they belonged with the other kids. After talking with their youth pastor, Rosie and Jim decided to visit Bridge Church. The church quickly became family, and Rosie began serving in the nursery.

At ABIDE and Bridge, Rosie found a place that not only ministered to her children, but fostered her passion for the underserved. A growing discontent grew in Rosie. She wanted to live with intentional purpose by serving those at the greatest risk. Rosie left her job and large salary to move into the inner city and live in an ABIDE-owned Lighthouse.

ABIDE began work in the Prospect Village neighborhood by taking on the house the neighbor kids knew as "danger" because of the condemnation sign hanging on the front window. Through volunteers and funds from a partner church, the house was refurbished and became home to Rosie and her family.

Rosie hit the ground running in her adopted neighborhood, starting a Bible study with several people who were not Christ followers. Through Rosie's leadership, some of these members began a neighborhood association which expanded to include neighbors from many blocks. The association has since partnered with the city to tear down dilapidated houses and provide grants to homeowners to fix up houses.

Jim and Rosie's impact was never felt more than in the wake of a tragedy in their neighborhood. A drive-by shooting that took the life of three young people occurred a few blocks from their Lighthouse. Jim and Rosie were out of town when they heard the news, but they came back that night to provide doughnuts and help neighbors process the tragedy. They prayed with neighbors at a prayer vigil and organized a neighborhood watch group, becoming a liaison between the police and the neighborhood.

Not only has ABIDE changed this neighborhood community by transforming the "danger" house, Lighthouse missionaries have provided light to a community that was mired in darkness.

Our neighbors are desperate for hope. People are dying around us in senseless tragedies. Jesus wept for Jerusalem. Do our hearts break for our neighbors? Do we cry out for our city?

The grassroots neighborhood approach breaks the overwhelming problems of the inner city into tangible, bite-sized pieces. Christians take ownership, and the church is mobilized to permeate the culture.

The spiritual gets practical when Christians get out of the seats. And the practical turns powerful when Christians get into the streets and make a difference in the world around them.

Simple, yet profound.

BUILDING A CULTURE OF LOVE

Transforming neighborhoods doesn't happen in a day. Transformation happens daily. The constant presence of ABIDE Lighthouses in neighborhoods builds a comprehensive culture of love that changes lives. Lighthouse families establish permanent roots in the inner city community, living out their faith and modeling a healthy lifestyle based on God's principles. Impressionable young lives are influenced more through loving relationships than through a program or classroom teaching.

Programs are only as good as the health of a child. Kids not only need a better program, they need a better childhood. Kids thrive when they develop nurturing relationships weaving in and out of their life experiences.

Doing life together is the heart of culture building. Lighthouse neighbors Zeke and Jeremy, 11-year-old twins, are proof of this life change. When ABIDE first met the brothers in 2011, their mother would not allow them to open the door, so volunteers left a plate of cookies at the front door as part of ABIDE's monthly outreach activities.

Over the next several years, four young ladies living in the neighborhood Lighthouse connected with the twins through music and skateboarding.

Finding common ground immediately built a level of trust with the boys. Soon the brothers began to stop by the Lighthouse to hang out, get a ride to Bridge Church, play piano or guitar, or join the young ladies for a weekend lunch. This led to a connection with the boys' parents and an invitation to the twins' birthday celebration.

The same connections happened as Twany and I opened our home to kids in our neighborhood. We'd take several vanloads to church, then bring the group home for Sunday dinner. Soon our house was brimming with 60-80 kids every Sunday afternoon. Some of our kids' best friends hung out at our house so often, they became a part of our family. Kaveon, one of the regulars, told me coming to our house was like going to Disneyland because we shared meals and had a lot of fun together. Amazing, isn't it? God can use the simplest acts of love in powerful ways.

Because ABIDE builds a culture of love with relationships at the center, lasting change occurs. These relationships support inner city kids in overcoming the culture of poverty and empowering them to grow in their God-given potential. Sharing a meal together or a simple plate of cookies can make a difference for kids like Zeke, Jeremy and Kaveon when paired with caring Christians living alongside their neighbors.

CHAPTER
11

COMMUNITY BUILDING EVENTS AND FAMILY SUPPORT PROGRAMS

DON'T MENTION JESUS

When I led our first team into the inner city to clean up the neighborhood around the ABIDE office, my instructions brought surprise. "Do not tell anyone about Jesus."

Someone frowned. "But that's not Christian."

I put on my work gloves. "The Bible says we should always be ready to give an answer for the hope that lies within us," I explained myself. "But we don't want to give answers until someone asks us a question."

More volunteers returned the following weekend to mow lawns and pick up trash as a second team worked on renovating the house ABIDE had purchased. We continued to show up and began to invite the neighbors to grill-outs, never sharing our hope until someone asked a question.

From those early moments onward, our attempts to share our faith were no longer a pushy or awkward presentation of the gospel. The natural process of sharing our hearts came when we connected relationally with our neighbors. It didn't take long before people had questions.

In one of our first outreaches between ABIDE and Bridge Church, a neighbor came outside as we mowed his lawn.

"Who are you again?" he asked.

"Bridge Church."

Shock and confusion crossed the man's face. "I didn't know churches did anything."

Wow. What a statement.

HOW NOT TO HAVE A BLOCK PARTY

Before the neighborhood approach, my first community outreach attempts fell pathetically short. I got up on some makeshift pulpit in the park to adamantly, and often loudly, ask people to give their lives to Jesus while Christian music played in the background. Many of my church friends considered me courageous, but my approach repelled unchurched people. Fewer and fewer people showed up each month.

When I sought advice from my pastor friends, they assumed people didn't care about the things of Christ. None of them questioned my tactics. They believed the people were the problem. Rather than change my approach, I stopped doing outreaches until years later.

When I took the time to get to know my neighbors through ABIDE's neighborhood approach, some of these "unchurched" people gave me a different view. They seemed honestly interested in God, but didn't appreciate the environments or vocabularies that came with church.

Instead of expecting my neighbors to change, I realized I needed to change. As the ABIDE team revisited the value of block parties, our goal was to connect with our neighbors and recast the vision of a vibrant and thriving community in the inner city. The old mentality was "work hard, get an education, and move out of the inner city," but the inner city had a rich culture that needed to be celebrated. ABIDE desired to use the block party as a tool to help rebuild the community.

ABIDE strives to build morale in the inner city while having fun through block parties and other community events. As momentum builds and the sense of community grows, people begin to think in terms of transforming rather than transferring out of the inner city.

Block parties which are hosted throughout the year now feature Motown music, free food, face painting, a petting zoo, bounce houses and other fun activities for families to enjoy together. The three-legged races and egg toss are a hit. Smiles and laughter abound. The first block party brought 125 people. Eight summers later, 2,500 children and families attended.

Many are incredulous. "A church is putting on this block party?"

We nod, adding that we only meet for an hour during Sunday church service. Again, people are surprised.

As people begin to reconsider church, they are more likely to show up at a Bridge Sunday service where we are intentionally sensitive to the unchurched. After people experience the fun and relationships at a block party, the possibility opens for an encounter with God.

MARQUITA

Marquita was a good student until a fateful night in junior high when a family friend sexually assaulted her and ripped away her innocence. The once outgoing young lady retreated to the solitude of her room and music. The assault left Marquita empty and suicidal.

School became an afterthought, and the once honor roll student barely passed any classes. By the end of her sophomore year, Marquita had virtually no credits.

Her friend Janaya, a part of the Bridge Church family, invited Marquita to come to church multiple times only to be rejected. Marquita had tried church in the past, but her faith did not protect her from being raped, so she was done with God.

Marquita finally relented when Bridge Church threw a block party. The activities reminded her of the fun she enjoyed as a little girl, and she grinned when I wished her a Merry Christmas in the middle of the summer. Janaya invited Marquita to youth night the following Tuesday, but she refused to go.

Janaya would not give up. When she offered Marquita twenty dollars to come to youth night, the easy opportunity to make money persuaded Marquita. As soon as Marquita stepped foot into Bridge Church, the youth pastor's words spoke directly to her. She loved the fun, positive atmosphere and confessed to Janaya, "I didn't know church could be like this."

One Tuesday night turned into consistent attendance on youth nights and then Sunday morning service. Marquita found hope in a new identity. No longer was she a victim. She was God's daughter. The next school year showed this new hope. Marquita began the long road to graduation needing to complete four years' worth of credits in two years.

While making gains in school, Marquita also grew at church. She served in a variety of ministries and developed in her leadership, eventually becoming a leader during youth night services.

With minimal tutoring and some help paying for a couple of night classes, Marquita graduated on time with her high school diploma. She enrolled at a local Christian university and completed two internships with ABIDE and Bridge Church. Today she is a leader at her university and a leader in north Omaha.

Marquita's story of sexual abuse and violence is common in the inner city. Recently, the facilitators of a workshop in which ABIDE participated asked 25 young ladies to speak of the violence they had seen. Like Marquita, every one of these young ladies had experienced past sexual abuse. These women are in desperate need of the positive love of Jesus Christ, but many won't come to church. As a church, we need to provide venues of love like block parties to help the hurting take the first steps of healing.

FOUNDATIONAL POVERTY VERSUS ECONOMIC POVERTY

Working in the inner city has given me insight into two types of poverty—economic and foundational. Education, employment and housing make up three factors in the pathway out of poverty, but focusing on economic poverty factors alone does not bring significant change.

Foundational poverty plagues the inner city. Broken family networks damage character development and moral fabric normally established in a family environment. When work ethic and similar values are not instilled in children, this lack will prevent lasting change if overlooked.

ABIDE focuses on foundational poverty by rebuilding the moral fabric in the inner city through community building events and family support programs. By providing a support network that a healthy family normally provides, and by including opportunities not available otherwise, we encourage, equip, and empower individuals to become leaders.

When ABIDE works with kids on a regular, sustainable basis in their own neighborhoods, they gain ground on foundational poverty issues. Children begin to understand their lives matter which births purpose and a desire to better themselves. Once the foundational factors of hope and internal drive are established, the issues of economic poverty can then be addressed.

Relationships are at the Heart

Connecting with neighborhood schools also allows more opportunities to serve. The principal at one inner city school needed volunteers to read to kids, so volunteers from ABIDE showed up. Most kids didn't have worthwhile extracurricular activities, so ABIDE and Bridge started a basketball program that attracted 200 students.

After a year and a half, the principal's assistant and her husband decided to visit Bridge Church because of our presence at the school. Not only did they surrender to Jesus, they ripped up their divorce papers and were baptized. Later, after the assistant invited the principal to Bridge, the principal gave her life to Jesus and got baptized on the school's empty lot in a special, open air service. Now the principal's assistant and her husband live in a Lighthouse.

In addition to the basketball program, tutoring serves as another touch point between Bridge volunteers and inner city youth. Children from kindergarten through sixth grade attend the after-school program at ABIDE's community center on 33rd Street where they receive a meal, get help from volunteer tutors, and work on life lessons.

Whether the focus is basketball, after-school tutoring, or job skill development, relationship building is at the heart of ABIDE's approach. We *connect* with neighbors relationally, *care* for them tangibly, and *call* them to take the next step with Jesus. Process is stressed over program. Educational success and skill development are secondary goals to the primary goal of connecting kids and families to Jesus. Spiritual development is the ultimate measure of our success. Without eternal hope, our temporary goals can only achieve temporary hope and short-term change.

ABIDE:
BRIDGE CHURCHES

CHAPTER

12

CHURCH IMPACT

More Than Temporary Hope

Brokenness, pain and suffering didn't become personal until I got closer to the problems in my city. As I began to minister to needs in the inner city, the struggles and stories caused me to weep with my neighbors. When I experienced God's heart for the broken, the pain broke my heart. As I examined the existing church model through these new lenses, I knew things needed to change.

My neighbors needed more than temporary hope and short-term change. They needed a lifeline of support that surrounded them from childhood to adulthood. While God used me to intervene before Markus committed suicide, Markus needed more. The same was true for Geno. He made progress after God prompted me to rescue him from the bar at midnight, but then returned to drugs when he moved and left the influence of the church family. Even Jake who accepted Christ and lived with my family for almost a year, had a much bumpier road when he lost his regular connection with other Christians.

In all three men, old habits surfaced too easily, and dysfunction returned. Leading them to Christ was the easy part. Developing disciples took more work and required help and encouragement from other radical world-changers. Church makes us stronger—we are better together.

My good works, if linked to a family of Christians, could empower the Markuses, Jakes and Genos on a pathway to a whole new future where the gospel transformed hearts and souls. Everyone involved would experience change. Changed people could then be used to change more people, and our city would be powerfully transformed.

GOOD WORKS VERSUS GOD'S WORK

A big difference exists between good works and God's work. The Bible pairs good works with kingdom building. Paul writes in Colossians 3:17, "Let every detail in your lives—words, actions, whatever—be done in the name of the Master, Jesus, thanking God the Father every step of the way." (MSG) Good works bring temporary results. God's work brings people to repentance and eternal hope.

My good works with the nonprofit, programmatic approach produced little lasting fruit. I took a hard look at nonprofits, including faith-based, and saw how very few considered their mission beyond the temporary. Housing programs provided affordable homes—why? Volunteers tutored children so kids would graduate and get good jobs. For what purpose? To move out of the inner city and miss out on impacting the environment? All the various programs, including mine, while admirable, had no eternal implications until the church got involved. The longer I served in the inner city, the more passionate I became about connecting people to a network of lifelong support.

Good works follow a person's faith in Jesus Christ, but the reversal of this equation means connecting those good works back to faith. Faith and good works, in its pure gospel form, are eternally linked together. Disjointing faith from good works is simply a humanitarian act of goodness. God wanted me to build a bridge where faith, hope and love interlock. That's the full gospel equation.

The more I considered good works versus God's work, the more I realized the significance of the local church and its power to impact my neighbors in the inner city. By my programmatic approach, I could only offer so much. The church, on the other hand, had a comprehensive approach and a wide array of people and resources that could more fully reach my neighbors, helping them take next steps in their development.

My definition of discipleship was narrow before working in the inner city. I didn't fully grasp the need for an ongoing network of support once people surrendered their lives to Jesus. To expect people who had been hurt so deeply to function normally was unreasonable. Deeply embedded thoughts needed to be rewired and plugged into God's word, and behaviors needed to be retrained. The old me judged a new Christian according to behavior, but dysfunction didn't disappear the moment someone surrendered to Christ. Wounds took time to heal. The deeper the wound, the longer the time to heal. Therefore, I needed to stop trying to decide if the internal change was authentic or not. Only God could judge the heart. Rather I needed to walk alongside new believers and help strengthen them in the broken places and train them for life. Discipleship is a lifelong journey, not a sprint. The church was needed from "womb to tomb."

A NEGATIVE VIEW OF CHURCH

One day I wondered what came to mind when people heard the word "church." This question became the focus of a survey in the inner city done by our team at ABIDE. The responses from over 300 adults disheartened me as a pastor.

Ninety percent of the respondents stopped attending church because of a negative experience. Many hadn't stepped inside a church since the ages of 10-12. Several described the church as totally disconnected from the real world and unrelated to their personal lives. Quite a few felt money given to fund the pastor's luxurious lifestyle was ridiculous. They didn't have the money to keep up with the fashion show on Sunday morning. Without hesitation, the respondents described church-goers as self-righteous. Frustration and anger were common. Despite the negative comments, however, most interviewees expressed appreciation that someone actually cared and listened to them.

The word *church* originated from the German word *kirche* which meant a place to go for a worship experience. Jesus used the word *ecclesia* to mean a people who gathered together and then scattered to accomplish a mission, but the meaning got lost in the German translation. The original word *ecclesia* often referred to soldiers who came together, got direction, and left for their mission. Over the years, however, *church* began to refer to a place rather than a people with a mission.

By IRS standards, a church can only perform worship service and activities. Defined by our culture today, church doesn't allow us to be a part of changing the world the way God calls us to do. This influenced me to start ABIDE as a nonprofit organization. In an ideal world where IRS rules didn't dictate the business of the church, I would never start another non-profit. God intended the church to lead the change, not the nonprofit. However, in American culture, we need a marriage of church and nonprofit.

CHRISTIANITY DEFINED

Defining Christianity determines the type of church we build. When Christians are seen as "radical world-changers," the focus highlights both our personal relationship with Jesus and our purposeful relationship with a broken world.

The word "radical" implies "getting back to the root or origin" of Christianity as defined in the scriptures. Romans 2:4 says, "God is kind, but He's not soft. In kindness He takes us firmly by the hand and leads us into a radical life-change." (MSG) Another translation says God's kindness leads to repentance. Radical change takes place in our lives when we recognize our need for a savior because of our sin. We invite Jesus to live inside us and become lord of our life—not just in an act of admission, but an act of submission—and everything radically changes. To paraphrase one Bridge member who got baptized, "God was always important to me, but when He became central in my life, everything changed to revolve around His plans for me."

"World-changer" comes from Acts 17:6 and refers to our purposeful relationship with Jesus and the broken world He came to save. Everywhere Paul and Silas traveled, they prayed for people, and lives were transformed and cities changed. City leaders accused them saying, "They have turned the world upside down (and) have come here, too." (NKJV)

We are changed by the gospel and called to change the world. Rethinking Christianity means rethinking church and its impact on the world.

Bridge Church started with a hunger to birth a multi-ethnic church focusing on connecting with the unchurched, individuals who have been hurt or disillusioned by the church, and those who needed a church. Our leadership team represented our desire—a family of believers with varying shades of skin. Through my consulting work developing leaders, I helped plant four other churches. Each started with the hope of reaching people far from Christ, but all became inward-focused within two years. Working with church leadership across the city, I'd seen the same pattern in most American churches. I longed for Bridge Church to buck the trend.

Walking through the doors of a church was easier fifty years ago because the surrounding culture mirrored many of its basic tenets. Prayer in public school was common while the Ten Commandments were prominently displayed in front of courthouses and other public places. Once American culture moved farther away from God, the church lost ground.

Not only did the church lose connection with today's culture, but we seem to have forgotten our mandate to influence the culture and impact the world. We enjoy other Christians, but forget those outside our walls when we stop engaging the culture. Sunday morning services, mid-week Bible studies and small groups become the predominant focus. The power of the local church fades because we are not lighting the darkness and penetrating the culture with the love, hope and faith of the gospel. If we're not intentional, our mission becomes simply to care for churched people rather than make disciples to transform a broken world.

SIZE AND IMPACT

A few months after we got involved in our first neighborhood cleanup project, Bryson who spent most of his time with our family, asked if he could come to our church. At that time, Bridge Church consisted of Tuesday night outreaches, but we had yet to begin Sunday morning services.

As I listened to my leadership team wrestle over styles of music and preaching that would make up a Sunday morning service, I interrupted the discussion to ask what would draw Bryson and other broken people to church. Our focus shifted, and we started the Sunday morning services with my son Jeremiah's best friend in mind. Our hearts connected with Bryson and the hurting in our neighborhood who needed a church family. Within five years, Bridge Church grew from 12 founding members to almost 500 formerly unchurched people who attend Sunday morning service where we regularly baptize people who surrender their lives to Christ.

The size of a church should complement its citywide impact. Sending capacity should be equally as important as our seating capacity.

Are we getting out of the seats?

We are called to be light and salt, Christians who are known in our city for our love and good deeds. While we do our part, Jesus calls people to Himself. As He says in Matthew 16:18, "I will build my church, and all the powers of hell will not conquer it." (NLT) Bridge Church dreams and works with like-minded churches to get out of the seats and into the streets.

CHAPTER

13

LOVE-HOPE-FAITH

LOVE IS THE ULTIMATE EXPRESSION OF OUR FAITH

God interrupted me one day while I read 1 Corinthians 13:13. I must've read the passage about faith, hope and love a thousand times, but this morning, a question popped off the page. Why did God consider love the greatest of these? Surely faith was the answer. After all didn't the book of Hebrews say it was impossible to please God without faith? I prayed and wrestled with this passage for two weeks in an effort to understand what God meant.

"Lord, I don't get this," I cried out, and He finally answered.

Ron, when you received me by faith, didn't you get a hope like never before that your life could be different?

I nodded in answer to the question which filled my spirit.

Doesn't that hope translate into actions of love, making love the ultimate expression of your faith?

"Thank you, Lord," I thought. "I like that."

The Lord spoke again. *Think back to the years before you became a Christ follower. Wasn't it love that drew you to me? Didn't you start to have hope that life could be different? As a result, didn't that hope lead you to receive me by faith?*

The revelation knocked the spiritual wind out of me. As a Christ follower, my faith gave me hope like I'd never known before which resulted in actions of love toward others. Before I chose to follow Jesus, however, seeing the loving actions of Christians gave me a vision of hope which resulted in steps of faith toward a life with Christ.

I'd never considered the complimentary principles of "faith, hope, love" and "love, hope, faith." For the Christ follower, the movement progressed from faith, to hope, to love. Whereas, for the non-Christ-follower, the movement flowed in the reverse, from love, to hope, to faith.

As I reflected on this newfound understanding, God continued to give me insight.

I know you love me, Ron, but you've been trying to reach people for me on the basis of faith. God paused as the words took meaning.

Stop reaching them on the basis of faith and focus on love. Love people, Ron. Engage them with love. You don't have to save people. I will draw all men to myself. Simply be prepared to give an answer for the hope that lies within you. I will save them.

This revelation changed my understanding of Christianity. I felt a new freedom to love people without condemnation. My place was not to judge or change them. I simply needed to love people. God would draw, save, and change them—not me.

BUILDING A BRIDGE OF HOPE

People try to make sense of the world through their five physical senses—sight, sound, smell, touch, and taste. Faith, however, is a *non*sense. Faith can't be grasped through any of the senses, so non-Christ-followers need a different approach to spiritual understanding. Love is the answer. God will draw them if I love them. Once He draws them, I need to be prepared to give an answer for my hope.

Love comes first. If we will lead with love, Jesus will draw people to Himself. The church should respond by loving our community in practical ways. Using tools like the murder map visually communicates the brokenness and challenges in our city and helps ignite a sense of passion and urgency around reaching out to people in our city.

Leaders can help awaken their congregations to the city's needs by focusing attention, affection and action toward a community of need that challenges people to live lives in complete submission to God. If we are going to transform the brokenness in our city, we as leaders must create consistent landing places so that our congregations might first be broken by what breaks the heart of God. God moves mightily when His people get out of the seats and into the uncomfortable and unfamiliar streets across our city.

Hope follows love. This is the hinging point for us as Christ-followers because it determines our motivation, intent and activity focus. Most people hope for a fulfilling job, a great education, or a good life. Our hope as Christians, however, is centered on a relationship with Christ which has eternal implications.

Faith connects people to Christ and His church family.

In all we do, we are the ones being changed. Discipling others means applying the truths of God's word into our everyday lives, making Jesus irresistible.

Leadership models how to share the gospel. When a congregation sees how a leader regularly gets involved and leads with love, they notice how Christ's love can be expressed in genuine and practical ways. When leaders aren't preachy or pushy, others realize they can do the same. They see us picking up trash and mowing lawns and recognize a degree in biblical studies isn't necessary. The spiritual becomes practical and simple to follow.

PUTTING THE UNCHURCHED FIRST

When we go door to door to hand out cookies, we not only invite families to join our programs for kids and adults, we ask if we can pray for them. For those who don't want prayer, we lessen the awkwardness with a smile and a jovial request to pray for a family dog or cat. Lightening the atmosphere opens most residents to share a prayer request.

Our prayers are typically short—maybe 10-15 seconds in duration—and avoid churchy words. While we truly hope for people to surrender their lives to Jesus, we recognize we need to be changed as much as anyone else.

Living intentionally for Jesus is so fulfilling and rich. Jesus is the one saving people—not us. We simply need to love people and always be prepared to give an answer for our hope. When people are ignited with hope, we can then connect them into the local church as the disciple-making organization God designed.

At Bridge Church, people can belong before they ever believe. They do not have to surrender to

Christ before exploring what surrender means. This is possible because leadership at Bridge intentionally models loving the unchurched at church. Leadership puts the needs of the unchurched above serving the needs and desires of the regular church-goers. The more that happens, the more church people understand that church isn't about them.

Years after serving in several neighborhoods, we approached a woman's house as she got home from work. Before she hurried inside, she turned toward our team. "I know who you guys are. You're Bridge Church. You're the ones who make it hard for people to say no to Jesus."

Wow. She summed up our hope to be light and salt. The church really becomes powerful when we get out of the seats and into the streets.

ESTABLISHING A HOPE VENUE WITHIN THE CHURCH

Hope is at the center of both equations, linking faith and love. The bridge of hope spans the divide between love and faith and builds a pathway to God.

To flesh out the idea of love-hope-faith, our leadership at Bridge began to discuss how to implement connections between the three concepts. We were most familiar with the Sunday morning church service as a venue of faith, but for the unchurched like Bryson, the step from love to faith was too big a leap without the venue of hope. Frustration would result, leading to an even wider chasm. How could Bryson go from being loved at a block party to experiencing faith at church?

The more we prayed and discussed this, the more we realized that we needed to establish a hope venue, not another faith venue. Our love venues—block parties, neighborhood clean-ups, and other outreaches—engaged non-believers. But we needed a bridge of hope to link love and faith. Bridge Church had to create a venue of hope if we wanted the unchurched to explore following Jesus.

Church is the answer, the hope of the world. But not church like I'd "done church" in the past. The "already convinced" had enough information. They were well fed, but maybe not well led. I couldn't keep huddling in faith venues like worship services, Sunday school classes and Bible studies while the world around me died. We needed to bridge love and faith, so Bridge started by making Sunday morning church service a venue of hope.

Sunday morning service at Bridge Church is a "come as you are" hope venue. The service is a great transition opportunity for the unchurched to engage with Christians in a life-lifting way. Music is joyful, high-energy and celebratory. Sermons encourage the unchurched to take the next step of faith while Bridge members connect in relationship.

CREATING A CULTURE OF HOPE WITHIN THE CHURCH

So how do we create a hope culture within the church where the unchurched feel valued and engaged? How do we build churches that create a bridge to God?

Christians must start with personal passion and ownership if the goal is to reach lost people. We need to look past unhealthy behaviors to people. Unruly kids or disrespectful adults don't know the unwritten rules if they've never been inside a church. Life is messy, and the church has to embrace the messiness for authentic transformation to take place. Jesus washed dirty feet and healed unclean lepers. Radical world-changers need to roll up our sleeves and get a little dirty. As leaders we need to sacrifice our preferences and start where lost people are if we're ever going to impact them.

Creating a culture of hope won't happen accidentally. Leadership must model expected behavior and lead the congregation with hands on training, so they can be mobilized to train others and multiply the effect through the entire church.

One expectation at Bridge is the "three minute rule." The first three minutes before and after service, our people are expected to greet and get to know new people. Leaders model the four "h's"—high fives, handshakes, heartfelt conversations, and side hugs so that church people get out of their comfort zones and begin welcoming and engaging the unchurched.

Bridge Church has also intentionally implemented other actions to create a culture of joy and vibrancy. Our goal is for children to have the best hour of their week at church. Upbeat music lifts spirits, including a disc jockey who plays music in the parking lot while our wave team greets people driving by as well as those entering the building. We want to make everyone feel valued, loved and welcome. All of this takes place before the hour-long service even begins. We want to create a "celebration before the celebration."

Remember the street children in Africa? When I realized beliefs were more formed than informed, my preaching changed, too. A sermon was not enough. My focus changed from "informing" people to "forming" Christ in people. I was mindful of the words, not assuming my audience knew the church lingo. My sermons were filled with real life stories, tangible action steps, and followed with landing places for people to practice their beliefs alongside the church leadership.

Bridge Church implemented three faith venues—small groups, one-on-one discipleship, and Bridge nights of worship—for believers ready to own their faith and train to be radical world-changers. Faith venues allow for faith to deepen while adding accountability and discipleship. As people connect with each other in small groups, they are encouraged to grow in both the areas of *tending* and *extending*. Participants study the Bible together twice a month and serve alongside one another in neighborhoods the remaining two weeks. This helps group members balance growth in their personal relationship with Jesus and propels them into the streets in a purposeful relationship with Jesus.

THAT'S A CHURCH I COULD JOIN

Recently a member of one of Bridge's partner churches had some issues with a boss that didn't "do" church. Her boss couldn't understand why she didn't like to work on Sundays. When her boss catered an event for ABIDE, he heard about the murder map and the mission to transform the inner city one neighborhood at a time.

He was dumbfounded and later confided in her. "I get why you go to church now. That's a church I could be a part of."

Real people want real answers to why faith should matter. If unchurched people are going to experience the good news of Jesus Christ, Christians have to get out of the seats and into the streets to do something that makes a difference.

Love really opens hearts. Hope bridges the gap. And faith transforms lives and neighborhoods.

DOMINICK

Dominick was a young man consumed with anger due to an unstable home life. Multiple men came and left, including a favorite who died of sleep apnea at his house. The instability pushed Dominick and his brother Tyron to find male role models on the streets, so the two boys joined gangs early in life.

Dominick teetered on the edge of prison or death. Early in his high school career, Dominick got expelled from school for a fight that fractured his cheek bone. About the same time he connected with Bridge Church through his younger brother Bryson.

Because of our neighborhood presence, Dominick came to church looking for something to do. He had to be restrained on multiple occasions for starting fights. Whenever anger consumed Dominick, his eyes would go blank and expressionless like he was possessed. He became a different person when his anger exploded.

I connected Dominick with a Christian school dedicated to giving individualized care to kids who didn't succeed in public schools. Dominick continued to attend church and built relationships that kept him away from friends in the gang.

Then a perfect storm hit Dominick's life.

His mother was incarcerated for an assault in a bar fight. With the stability of his mother taken from the family, Grandma moved in and began caring for Dominick and his four siblings.

One afternoon Dominick visited Roscoe, a friend who lived on the corner of our block. Over the years I'd tried to connect with Roscoe, but he chose to join a gang because of family ties. His mental challenges made him an easy target. When the gang needed a fall guy, Roscoe was their man.

Minutes after Dominick headed home, a car screeched around the corner, and the driver shot Roscoe. Roscoe's last words rang through the neighborhood as the EMTs loaded him onto the stretcher. "I don't want to die. I don't want to die. I don't want to die."

Roscoe died at the hospital at age 16. Dominick vowed to live differently and committed his life to Jesus because of his friend's death. He went on a short-term mission trip with Bridge Church to El Carmen, Mexico, a small town outside of Monterrey. While there, Dominick asked for prayer from the team. After the prayer, Dominick shared, "It feels like something is coming out of me."

He returned to the inner city with a new lease on life. The anger that once consumed Dominick had subsided. He took on leadership roles at Bridge Church and graduated. Dominick worked on employment skills with ABIDE's staff and landed his first job.

Through Bridge Church's comprehensive love, hope and faith approach, Dominick has had a supporting church family who stood by him through all the ups and downs. The bridge of love, hope and faith resulted in Dominick coming to Christ and succeeding at work.

ABIDE:
INVEST IN LEADERS

14

DEVELOPING RADICAL LEADERS

MYRON

Myron lived with his father, a pimp, and his mother, a prostitute, in the projects across the street from what would eventually become Bridge Church. He joined a gang and found trouble at an early age. After multiple run-ins with the law, Myron and his friends robbed a business owner. When the owner fought back, Myron attempted to fire his gun only to have the trigger jam. He scattered with the rest of the gang members, but ran into an off-duty police officer who arrested him. His friends escaped.

Myron called his grandmother. "I screwed up again." He couldn't hold in his emotions. "I'm so sorry. I love you." Her consolation echoed in his ears as he called his girlfriend to break off their relationship because he faced 200 years in prison.

He hung up and fell to his knees, weeping. "God, if you change me, I'll serve you."

Myron received a reduced sentence, but he still faced 35 years in jail. As he served his time, God filled Myron with His love. The guards regularly tested Myron for drugs, sure chemicals were the reason for his joy. He spoke words of destiny over the other inmates and repeated the words of Jeremiah 29:11 aloud as he looked into the mirror in his cell. "'For I know the plans I have for you,' declares the Lord, 'plans to prosper you and not to harm you, plans to give you hope and a future."' (NIV) Myron got his GED and enrolled in classes in an online Christian college. God granted Myron favor when his sentence was further reduced and he was sent to a work release facility.

Meanwhile, I had been praying that God would send a young African-American leader who had experienced the hardships of the inner city to help us at ABIDE and Bridge. A few weeks later, Kristin who'd been coming to Bridge for several years, wanted her boyfriend to share his testimony. Within weeks, 25-year-old Myron joined the ABIDE/Bridge staff, and I began mentoring him every week as he finished his work release program. Our staff testified at Myron's parole hearing, and he was granted parole.

God answered my prayer. Myron's joy and instant connection with youth grew the Bridge youth group from 40 to 200. He finished his degree in pastoral studies and married Kristin. The two now have three children, and Myron serves as a leader on the team of pastors at Bridge. Though Myron had many opportunities to leave the inner city, he chose to stay as a leader and transform the neighborhood where he grew up and minister to the needs within his community.

LEADERS DRIVE CHANGE

Leaders drive change in a community. People will follow leaders whether the leaders are positive or negative. The overwhelming mantra to "work hard, get an education, and move out of the inner city" has led to the flight of many leaders from the community. The remaining negative leaders influence the younger generation to turn to gangs, drugs, and crime.

Generational violence cannot be underestimated. Without intervention, the culture of violence will only grow. Frequent exposure to violence, fear and grief disrupts healthy development and makes kids vulnerable to traumatic stress. When kids don't feel secure, self-hatred, distrust, and insecurity result. Moral values shatter, including the ethics of caring.

"Outsiders" who stand on the sidelines and propose changes to a community where they don't live or serve perpetuates distrust and further alienates the community from taking the lead. Revitalizing the inner city starts with developing leaders from within the community through mentoring and hands on training.

Developing radical leaders is at the heart of both ABIDE and Bridge Church. Through internships and leadership development programs, our focus is raising leaders who can lead where God directs.

Kids' Club started as an outreach for first through third graders, but changed to focus on fourth through sixth graders. For four weeks during the summer, ABIDE/Bridge exposes kids to opportunities not readily available to them. The young leaders visit colleges and the library, take field trips to shadow jobs, serve on Lighthouse projects, and make presentations to ABIDE church partners.

The summer internship program is open to high school graduates and college students. They live in a Lighthouse over the summer and serve in various ways while studying leadership books to develop their skills as leaders.

Financial barriers can prevent those in the inner city from exploring God's calling for their lives. To help overcome these obstacles, ABIDE raises funds to invest in these leaders by providing a job on staff at ABIDE/Bridge where they are mentored by other staff members in addition to getting practical hands on experience and exposure to different resources as they grow as leaders.

Through ABIDE's neighborhood approach, many young people are mentored by Lighthouse residents and others in the Bridge family. One of the maintenance leaders at Bridge connected with a neighbor boy named Antoine, and the impact has been powerful as the young man has grown into a strong leader.

ANTOINE

By age 12, Antoine's life spiraled in the wrong direction. One of 26 children on his father's side, Antoine hardly connected with his father who breezed in and out of his life. He lived with his mother and sisters in a household full of dysfunction, chaos and drama. Anger and resentment built inside him, threatening to erupt.

His family moved from rental to rental with little to eat most days. Constant fighting between Antoine's mom and sisters reverberated through the walls. When his friends invited Antoine to an ABIDE work project renovating a Lighthouse, followed by a night at Family Fun Center, he felt a rush because he finally had an outlet for his anger.

For the first time in his life, he connected with people who cared. Through this experience, Antoine got involved in ABIDE's community building events and family support programs. He brought his homework to the Learning Center and turned around his failing classes. Instead of getting suspended, Antoine stayed in school. When he lost a cousin through gang violence, Antoine didn't retaliate despite pressure from his family and friends. The relationships at Bridge enabled him to resist this strong pull to regain respect. This showed huge growth for Antoine, considering just months earlier, he had to be restrained when friends urged him into a fight.

Antoine began helping on other Lighthouse projects. Working alongside ABIDE's maintenance director, Antoine found an outlet for his pain and anger. Antoine loved working with his hands and learning new skills. The maintenance director treated Antoine as a leader, and he rose to the expectation. Hearing he could do great things in life helped Antoine focus on his goals rather than the next fight.

Antoine's story isn't over. His life changed course thanks to ABIDE's intervention and relational approach. For young people whose lives have been filled with trauma and dysfunction, ABIDE develops leadership in a steady, consistent environment of love.

15

RELEASING
EMERGING LEADERS

CHURCH LEADERSHIP

The Bible's leadership model for maturing Christians can be found in Ephesians Chapter 4 which describes five leadership roles: shepherd, teacher, apostle, prophet, and evangelist. All five roles are designed to equip radical world-changers for acts of ministry to the broken world around them.

The shepherd cares for and equips people to compassionately support the needs of hurting people. The teacher brings insight and draws out wisdom from scripture. The best teachers don't teach for the sake of knowledge. Rather, they equip people with opportunities to grow closer to Jesus in order to live out a purposeful relationship and impact others.

The apostle blazes new trails by pushing the people to the next mountain. The apostle challenges the people to get out of the seats and into the streets in order to make a difference in the world.

The prophet acts as a compass helping people stay strong in their relationship with Jesus while also sacrificing their lives for others. The prophet challenges the church and calls out the other leaders whenever a course of correction is needed.

The evangelist models how to share one's faith. This leader also provides landing spots for Christians to practice sharing their faith with their neighbors.

If all five types of leaders are actively pursuing their gifts, the church doesn't turn inward. Instead, rhythm is achieved between ministering to those inside the walls and reaching those outside the walls of the church.

In my experience consulting with leaders from multiple churches, leadership in the American church today is centered on the shepherd and teacher. I did the same when I helped plant four other churches before Bridge. I largely ignored the *extending* leaders—the apostle, evangelist, and prophet—and focused more on *tending* to the church members through shepherding and teaching.

Rather than strategically position leadership, churches often push those gifted in *extending* roles into *tending* roles like Sunday school teachers or Bible study facilitators. As a result, many apostles, evangelists and prophets have started nonprofits to push for change without the backing of a local church. Ephesians 4 should be the model for building the leadership in our churches.

Just like the physical body has many systems, including the respiratory, cardiovascular and skeletal systems, which enable the body to function, a healthy church has three systems: tending, extending, and sending. A healthy church should be birthing more healthy churches by sending its leaders to reclaim new territory. Reaching and raising up leaders isn't enough. The church needs to release leaders to do the work God has planned.

Like childbirth, birthing leaders is painful. As a leader, we watch over our spiritual children, allowing them to fail in the growing process. When the time comes to let go, our hearts feel the severing of the bonds formed over the years together. As much as we want to hold on, we have to trust God because He always has bigger plans.

Raising leaders to be released requires a kingdom mindset rather than a congregational mindset. Just like God reminded me that my kids are not my own, the leaders under me are not my leaders. Like my children, these leaders have been given to me for a season, to be released when the time is right.

At ABIDE and Bridge Church, God is asking us to send out leaders in faith even before other leaders have stepped forward to fill the missing roles. When that leads to sleepless nights, God wants me on my knees asking Him to raise up emerging leaders He wants to use during the new season.

God's plans are always bigger than ours. Recently an opportunity opened to plant ABIDE/Bridge in another state. This means releasing three strong leaders and their families to move. While this isn't easy, kingdom advancement means letting go and letting God.

LETTING GO

The real test in letting go came when I stepped down as CEO of ABIDE and relinquished the lead pastor role of Bridge. I watched young leaders emerge and knew the time had come to let go. If I didn't let young leaders step up, they would leave, and I wanted ABIDE and Bridge to flourish under their leadership.

My son Josh received a basketball scholarship to play for Creighton University in Omaha after high school. He joined the team and worked hard, wanting to leave the inner city behind when he graduated. The fear of constant danger wore on Josh, and he figured basketball was his ticket out of the place where he'd grown up.

A knee injury as a freshman changed his perspective. By his sophomore year, Josh decided to pursue God's dream over his own when he sensed God asking if he was willing to serve Him 110%.

The next year Josh married Jennifer, a girl he met at Bridge Church, and they moved into a single room at ABIDE to wait for God's direction.

Myron lived in the basement at the time, so the two began working out together at the gym and formed a strong bond. Despite the differences in their upbringing, Josh admired Myron's contagious faith and the obstacles he'd overcome.

A month later, Dominick's friend, Roscoe, was gunned down at the corner of our street. His last words rang through the neighborhood as the EMTs loaded Roscoe onto the stretcher. "I don't want to die. I don't want to die. I don't want to die."

The shooting impacted Josh in much the same way as the murder of Carissa and Chloe affected me. Josh stared at the face in the casket and saw the young boy who once ran up and down our street. Even in death, Roscoe held no peace. Gang members filed past the body, vowing revenge or breaking down with grief. Josh could almost hear God's audible voice. *What role can you play in the lives of young men like Roscoe?*

God ignited my son's affection for the brokenness around him through the death of this

16-year-old kid. Like me, Josh imagined a future living elsewhere, but God called him to advance the work of ABIDE and Bridge Church in the inner city.

When Josh graduated with a degree in public relations, he turned down an incredible career and opportunity to play basketball overseas. A few months' pledge to work with ABIDE/Bridge has since turned into a long-term commitment.

Josh and Jennifer eventually moved into the Fowler Lighthouse where the two have committed to building a great city one neighborhood at a time. Today they have three children, Joshua, Joseph, and Julianna, who they are raising to be radical world-changers.

Josh admits that he never had the intention of leading ABIDE and Bridge Church, but he can see how God positioned him years before he could envision the dream. Josh has advanced the vision and provided strong leadership to ABIDE and Bridge.

ABIDE:
DIVERSITY

16

A PICTURE OF HEAVEN ON EARTH

THE PROBLEM WITH DIVERSITY

I looked over the black faces around me, excited with the possibilities to partner with 40 African-American pastors in the inner city.

"Well, as you can see," the pastor introduced me and nodded my way. "We have another white guy trying to do the same white thing in our community even though we all know it's not going to work."

So much for my grandiose plans for racial reconciliation. My heart plummeted as I took the stage, knees visibly knocking. The bluntness in the African-American culture jarred me.

I cleared my throat in an effort to regain my composure. Red flooded my pale flesh now beaded with sweat. "I, uh, wanted to ask for your support to advertise an upcoming pastors' conference."

The fliers I held out ruffled with the tremble in my hand. "Um, here's some information you can pass out to your leaders if you wouldn't mind."

I avoided eye contact and hurried off the stage. *What was I thinking? How could I ever hope to make a difference in the inner city if I couldn't scale the insurmountable racial tension separating whites and blacks?*

A Story of Two Rons

My friend Ron, who I lovingly call black Ron, often attends speaking engagements with me whenever I speak about racial reconciliation.

Black Ron admits to the crowd that he hated white people growing up in inner city Chicago. He believed white people had all the money, so the only way he could escape poverty was to steal from his enemy. As a result, black Ron spent time in and out of jail. An armed robbery landed black Ron in a cell awaiting trial. He attended a prison Bible study for the promise of free donuts and encountered God. That night, God gave black Ron an out-of-body experience where he saw his physical body crushed in a trash truck while his screams alerted a growing crowd. His old life was gone. God made black Ron a new creation.

Miraculously black Ron was acquitted and met a white business owner who offered him a job. He and his wife left the most violent housing project in Chicago and moved to a house in Sioux City, Iowa. For the first time in his life, black Ron encountered poor whites, and his experiences began to shift his beliefs. He moved to Omaha and became a prison chaplain. Soon black Ron's life crossed mine.

In front of the same audience, black Ron will stop his story while I begin mine. Until I—white

Ron—moved to the inner city, I blamed black people for the crime and violence in the city. White Ron critically judged black people as irresponsible and lazy. White Ron wished blacks would quit complaining. He took no responsibility for his part in the injustice, saying slavery had ended long ago.

While we are truly better together, these two Rons represent the problem of diversity. White Ron doesn't see his overwhelming "privilege" and accept responsibility for injustice while black Ron is stuck in anger and the frustration of "inferiority." He's tired of being taken advantage of, so black Ron isn't willing to work with white Ron because he's "been there, done that." Both Rons embody the dominant opinions of their individual communities. Until blacks and whites acknowledge both sides have responsibilities and a better future together, we won't be able to walk together because we can't even talk together.

THE POWER OF DIVERSITY

God is the creator of diversity. He made the beautiful array of skin tones and eye colors. He understands every language and knows every heart. Diversity can be a powerful picture of heaven on earth. The Bible says that every nation, tribe, people and language will make up heaven.

Shouldn't we strive for this on earth, worshipping together with all our brothers and sisters?

Radical world-changers belong to one church with many expressions, but ethnic and cultural barriers have kept the church from thriving in a divisive and conflicted world. The church must persevere through the challenges and build a multi-ethnic, multi-cultural, multi-generational family to break down barriers and become a citywide expression of the kingdom of God.

The power of diversity is essential in the church or the city won't be transformed by the gospel. If church members don't get along with each other, how can we expect diverse groups of people in our city to get along? Before Jesus was betrayed, his prayer in John 17 acknowledged diversity as He asked God to unite all believers so the world would believe. This prayer for diversity represents the heart of the King for the kingdom. He sent His son to die so that a broken world would find hope.

Ownership underlies the heart of the lingering conflict. In general, most white people in America don't see the hurt, damage, and injustice of racial conflict. Therefore, they don't take responsibility for the racial tension in society. Many blacks, on the other hand, are angry over the injustice and lack empathy or concern for whites. A vicious cycle is the result.

Imagine a baseball game where the home team is winning by a landslide. In the bottom of the seventh inning, the umpire discovers the home team has been cheating. The home team apologizes, the score stays the same, and the game resumes. Unfair, right?

The same thing has happened to African-Americans. For years, the dominant culture of white America has been cheating through slavery and injustice only to apologize late in the game. The score, however, never changed, so the minority community has struggled to level the playing field.

The emerging diversity movement is showing promise of change. Young people don't have to think about being white and black together because they've experienced diversity through school integration and cultural changes.

Jamison, a young leader at Bridge Church, exemplifies this. Though he was expected to take over the church his father pastored, Jamison felt disconnected to the all-black congregation. He'd played sports in high school with a diverse mix of kids, so he longed for the same mix of races in his church family. When Jamison could no longer live with the duality, he had to make a decision. He left his father's church and joined the leadership team at Bridge. The decision was the most heart-wrenching decision he'd ever made because his father disowned him. Through much pain, Jamison chose the kingdom value of diversity over his relationship with his earthly father. Incredible acts of courage are needed for the power of diversity to impact our world.

HOW TO BUILD KINGDOM DIVERSITY

So how do we build diversity? The church needs to rally a diverse group of people around the city so radical world-changers can impact the brokenness. Kingdom advancement must be the focus, not diversity. The church needs to move past choosing my culture (separation) and choosing your culture (assimilation) to *reconciliation*, choosing God's diverse culture. When the church embraces God's heart for the city, real needs intersect the gospel, and the church attracts diversity through working together.

Diverse leadership must be cultivated. We do this by intentionally recruiting diverse leaders, investing in them and broadening their sphere of influence. The old paradigm positions only the person in power with financial resources to distribute resources to others. This comes off as patronizing and paternalistic and doesn't value the giftedness of others. If the church does not cultivate a belief that everyone has something to offer, diverse leadership is stunted and eventually leaves.

The church must also cultivate a culture that attracts diversity. Language and music must connect with people's feelings and understanding. A celebratory atmosphere and freedom of expression encourages diversity. Location further matters. Capture diversity by considering the location in the city that most rallies diversity. Valuing diversity in communication should constantly be stressed. One of our top values at Bridge Church is that we are better together.

The emerging diversity movement in the church should be innovative and inclusive. Language should be life-lifting, highlighting the beauty of diversity. Conversations about the power of diversity can overshadow past baggage of ignorance and anger. Issues can then be approached from different angles, and reconciliation pursued over confrontation. Individuals discover their roles and voices when everyone humbly participates. The church should model that we are truly better together.

Demarco, an African-American and former gang member at Bridge, felt like an outsider at his wife's white church. People viewed him as needy and never as someone with something to offer. Because relationships are reciprocal at Bridge, everyone participates and has something to contribute. As a result, Demarco is now fully involved in church. The power of diversity can truly inspire, influence and transform our city.

CHAPTER

17

WHAT'S IMPORTANT

Radical DNA

Diversity doesn't work if we don't have the same DNA as our brothers and sisters in Christ. Surrender is at the heart of our call as Christians. It's easy to recognize our need for a savior, but far more difficult to give up control and surrender our lives to Jesus. Diverse radical world-changers need to be united under the same banner of love. Our skin tones may be varied, but our DNA should be the same—the DNA of our Father.

The DNA of Christians must reflect our call to be radical world-changers. We know God loves us just the way we are, but He loves us too much to let us stay that way. God wants to change us, grow us and use us to change the world. As we give up control and surrender our lives to Jesus, He begins a process of radical transformation that can be summed up in the following acronym:

Relentless for God
Abundant in Life
Diversity from Heaven
Identity in Christ
Called to the World
Advancing Christ's Kingdom
Life-lifting in heart, mind and actions

Because Christianity includes both a personal relationship and a purposeful relationship with Jesus, the DNA of a radical world-changer reflects both parts of our responsibility. Each of these characteristics fall into either tending our relationship with Jesus or extending our lives to others.

R: RELENTLESS FOR GOD

God's word in Matthew 6:33 says, "Seek first the kingdom of God and live righteously and He will give you everything you need." (NLT) When we are relentless, nothing will stop us. We strive hard after God. While work, family, school, and other priorities vie for our attention, nothing should outweigh seeking God and living completely for Him. The Bible says God will take care of every need and aspect of our lives if we put Him first. Above all else, radical world-changers have to create time and space to pursue God with relentless passion.

Relentless Christ-followers at Bridge move into Lighthouses where they give their lives to serving their neighbors. As they seek God first, other priorities take second place. Relentless pursuit of God transforms lives.

A: ABUNDANT IN LIFE

John 10:10 says, "I have come that they may have life, and that they may have it more abundantly." (NKJV) Abundance means having more than enough. We lack nothing. When Jesus begins to change us, our focus changes from temporal things we lack to the abundance of treasure we receive from our Father in heaven. Because of God's amazing love, radical world-changers have access to everything in heaven and on earth. We live in a new mentality of abundance, recognizing we are blessed to be a blessing. Rather than ask, "What can I get," we ask, "What can I give?" As radical world-changers, we have more than enough, and we love to give away what we have.

D: DIVERSITY FROM HEAVEN

We are better together. We need each other.

Diversity is a beautiful picture of heaven on earth in the way we love and relate with each other. Revelation 7:9 shows a glimpse into heaven. ". . . a great multitude that no one could count, from every nation, tribe, people and language, (stood) before the throne and before the Lamb. . ." (NIV)

Diversity isn't just something we appreciate. We should pursue diversity because diversity strengthens who we are as individuals and as a whole. Mother Theresa said, "I can do what you cannot do, and you can do what I cannot do, but together, we can do great things!" As a dynamic, diverse team of people, we accomplish so much more together. As radical world-changers, our heart is to see heaven become a reality on earth through the tangible reality of diversity united under the banner of Christ.

I: IDENTITY IN CHRIST

Who we are determines what we do. Identity is central to who we become. Because of sin, it's easy to lose our real identity in Christ and find our identity in our jobs, our family, even the mistakes we've made and the pain of our past.

Once we allow Jesus to lead us, however, He gives us a new identity. According to 2 Corinthians 5:17, "Anyone who belongs to Christ has become a new person. The old life is gone; a new life has begun!" (NLT) Radical world-changers get a fresh start, free from all other false identities. We become who He calls us to be.

C: Calling to Change the World

We are uniquely created for a specific calling. Jeremiah 29:11 says, "'For I know the plans I have for you,' declares the Lord, 'plans to prosper you and not to harm you, plans to give you hope and a future.'" (NIV)

Each of us is called to do something. Our gifts, passions and strengths help point to the call God has on our lives. Our calling acts as a compass, giving direction to our lives. Discovering our calling takes time as we process our identity and life experiences. Our calling as radical world-changers allows us to pursue life with purpose.

A: Advancing Christ's Kingdom

We are called to change the world by advancing the kingdom of God. He is at work everywhere, and He has called us to join Him in the work.

Jesus told His disciples in Matthew 9:37, "The harvest is great, but the workers are few." (NLT) We run into people at work, the gym, the store, or in our neighborhood whose hearts are ready to receive the love of Jesus. Radical world-changers ask God, "Where do you want me to help advance your kingdom today?"

L: LIFE-LIFTING IN HEART, MIND AND ACTIONS

We always build on the bright spots. Rather than focus on problems, we focus on being the solution. We build on what builds others up. As Ephesians 4:29 says, "Do not let any unwholesome talk come out of your mouths, but only what is helpful for building others up according to their needs, that it may benefit those who listen." (NIV)

When issues come between Christians—and they will—we go to God first. The cross is a picture of His plan for peace. Radical world-changers go vertical first—asking God for His love, forgiveness and direction—before going horizontally with one another.

We focus on what is good and pleasing and encourage others to reach their full God-given potential. No one is perfect, but the God of perfection is changing each one of us. Since He's the one changing us, we can be an instrument in His hand to speak life into one another. As radical world-changers, we always think the best and speak the best about others.

THE ULTIMATE GOAL

Looking back to the argument Twany and I had over the skin color of Kiesha's future husband makes me shake my head in embarrassment. Color didn't factor into Kiesha's decision of who she would marry. She fell in love with a Samoan named Peniamina, and the two became missionaries in Thailand.

Kingdom diversity has the same heart. Love trumps color. Radical world-changers fall in love with Jesus, and He changes us to reflect the DNA of the Father. Diverse people are united under His banner of love.

One strand of our DNA makeup reflects *who we are* as radical world-changers: **R**elentless pursuers of Jesus with **A**bundant life in a **D**iverse family of believers. Our **I**dentity in Christ is the glue holding this radical strand of DNA together with its counterpart. The second strand reflects *what we do* as radical world-changers: using our gifts and **C**alling to **A**dvance God's kingdom in **L**ife-lifting action. We are truly diverse, R-A-D-I-C-A-L world-changers united by the love of Jesus to make an impact in the world.

At Bridge, we strive for diversity with one objective in mind: kingdom advancement. We don't build diversity for the sake of diversity. At the heart of the kingdom of heaven are diverse, radical world-changers with the same DNA as the Father. Advancing the kingdom must be the focus of a purposeful relationship with Christ—this is the ultimate goal of diversity.

ABIDE:

ENGAGE PARTNERS—
WE'RE BETTER
TOGETHER

18

MULTIPLICATION

A GOD-SIZED VISION REQUIRES MULTIPLICATION OF CHURCHES

The day I stood in front of the two child-sized caskets containing the lifeless bodies of my two neighbor girls, something inside of me snapped. When God spoke to me, I was empowered with conviction that moves mountains. And yet, I felt overwhelmed and incapable of saving a single life. I became desperate, knowing I couldn't continue doing ministry alone. I needed to involve others in order to make the kind of difference that would transform the inner city for every child.

Thousands of inner city children need the love and nurturing of caring people. I needed a God-sized vision for my city—one that would sustainably change an entire community. I could no longer think in terms of my one life and my one congregation. I needed to unite with pastors and leaders from across my city to have a compelling God-sized vision for our city.

If Christians got involved, their hearts would break and passion would ignite, birthing action. A programmatic approach didn't produce lasting change, but churches could provide a comprehensive approach from "womb to tomb," connecting and impacting these children throughout their entire lives.

Desperation and multiplication go hand in hand.

Facing an unending list of problems in the inner city has fueled my desperation to see a multiplication movement of leaders and churches across America to bring Jesus and His kingdom to all parts of our city and world. Multiplication is not an option. The cost is too high. We have to multiply.

AN ARMY OF VOLUNTEERS

Roughly 7,500 volunteers a year have embraced the vision of multiplication as they log endless hours serving alongside ABIDE and Bridge Church. Seeing diverse individuals serve together is both humbling and inspiring. As one neighborhood after another gets adopted, the dream of no more inner city gets closer to becoming reality.

Don is a contractor who sees his business as a way to advance God's kingdom. For several years, he took a week off at Christmas to help with a refurbishment project. Not only did he pay his employees to help, he encouraged them to volunteer additional time and rallied other small businesses to help with everything from spraying for termites to installing countertops.

Larry is a demolition expert with a generous heart. He consistently volunteers and donates to the mission of ABIDE and Bridge. When he overheard Twany's dream of having a yard with grass, he showed up with a truckload of sod—a rarity in the inner city where yards become dumping grounds or lots to park cars.

Greg and Nancy own a large basement waterproofing and foundation repair business with hundreds of employees in multiple locations. After they heard about the mission of ABIDE and Bridge, they brought in their local employees to repair a collapsing basement on a Lighthouse duplex. At the completion of the project, Greg and Nancy hosted a block party and invited all the neighbors.

Age is not a deterrent to Dick who heads up a group of volunteers he lovingly calls the "geezers." Now in his 80s, Dick continues to bring a group of volunteers into the inner city each week—something he's done for 20 years. One year he involved several local contractors to train nearly two dozen inner city youth as they worked on a construction project. At the end of two weeks, those over age 18 received a job—a venture worth replicating in the future.

Thousands of other volunteers make a difference. Chris is a venture capitalist with a kingdom mindset who has footed the bill for several Lighthouses. Pete is a plumber who donates countless dollars of labor and then hands ABIDE a check instead of a bill. Harry is an HVAC guy who repairs and installs used systems people donate. He is always available to answer my after-hour calls. Without this army of volunteers, ABIDE and Bridge could not multiply the impact in the inner city.

ENGAGING PARTNERS

Risk-taking and faith venturing churches have also joined in the multiplication effort by becoming partners with ABIDE/Bridge. Since the renovation of the first two Lighthouses, many churches have followed. One partner church member donated a house because he was headed to Iraq on deployment with the military. Another church purchased two duplex units with proceeds from a creative event they sponsored. Today, the list of church partners continues to grow.

More than ever we recognize our need to partner with multiple churches, so ABIDE actively engages others across the city to adopt neighborhoods and multiply the principle of loving our neighbors. Partners sign an agreement with ABIDE, making a commitment in three areas—relating, serving, and giving.

Under the relating commitment, partners pledge to make monthly connections with neighbors. They also commit to connect with ABIDE/Bridge through a citywide missional network, quarterly administrative meetings, and annual relational luncheons.

With the serving commitment, partners make a weekly promise to serve inner city children, youth, and families in a variety of ways, including helping with Bible club, basketball, swimming, tutoring, or mentoring. Monthly commitments focus on projects and activities like mowing lawns and trash pick-up or community events like the block parties and holiday events.

Partners can further pledge monthly and annual financial donations and scholarships toward children, youth, and family programs, community events, and refurbishing houses.

ABIDE/Bridge is gaining a strong foothold in Omaha as a result of churches uniting. The impact is causing ripples to touch lives across our city with the love of Jesus. As an old African proverb says, "If you want to go fast, go alone. If you want to go far, go together." One young leader at Bridge is living proof that together is better.

A DIVINE INTERSECTION

Bobbie Jo dropped out of high school and ran away from home to escape the chaos and dysfunction of her mother's lifestyle and became pregnant by age 15.

Not long after the birth of her baby, Bobbie Jo witnessed an argument that would change her life forever. Like normal, her mother demanded money from Bobbie Jo's grandmother. Oftentimes Bobbie Jo's grandmother had to choose between paying for her medication or her mortgage, in addition to all the other household expenses on her $800 monthly budget.

As the argument unfolded, Bobbie Jo saw a future of disparity and hopelessness flash before her eyes. At that moment, she vowed to change the course of her life for the sake of her daughter. She enrolled in high school again, married the father of her daughter, took on responsibility to raise her 6-year-old sister and returned to her grandmother's church.

Bobbie Jo graduated with honors and received a full-ride scholarship to college where she got her degree in special education. She accepted a job at her high school alma mater with the goal to save money and provide a better life for her kids away from the inner city.

God had other plans. He intersected Bobbie Jo's life with an old neighbor who had an encounter with God after he got shot. The neighbor invited Bobbie Jo to Bridge Church. Soon, Bobbie Jo and her sister joined a Bridge team on a mission trip to Mexico.

I saw a strong leader in Bobbie Jo on this trip, so I cast a vision for her to transform her inner city neighborhood rather than transfer out of the community. She accepted a job at ABIDE, though it paid only half of her teaching salary, and joined our team as a new leader.

Bobbie Jo lived in the home where she'd grown up since her grandmother gave her the house upon her death. Hearing ABIDE's vision inspired Bobbie Jo to reach out to her neighbors. One of those neighbors, a lady named Jasmine, resisted Bobbie Jo's invitations to come to Bridge Church, but Bobbie Jo didn't give up. Finally Jasmine agreed to come to Bridge where she was overwhelmed with love and acceptance. When several Omaha churches partnered together for a community outreach, Jasmine invited her mother.

Multiplication of leaders and churches is God's strategy for overwhelming tragedy. Because of churches working together to serve alongside each other during this outreach, Jasmine and her mother connected with the people at Bridge Church.

Jasmine was Carissa and Chloe's older sister.

God had a miracle in the works.

CHAPTER

19

FULL CIRCLE

CHARGED WITH MURDER

The police eventually traced the murders of Carissa and Chloe to their oldest sister, Jasmine. A broken, scared teenager, Jasmine endured sexual abuse from an early age.

By ninth grade, Jasmine couldn't cope with the flashbacks from her abuse. She found every pill in the house and gulped them down, hoping she wouldn't wake up. When the plan failed, Jasmine kept the pain inside. Rather than tell anyone, she made plans to run away to California with her older boyfriend.

Carissa and Chloe stood in her way. Jasmine couldn't take her sisters with her to California, so she had to protect them from the house of horrors she'd experienced.

Mentally unstable from years of trauma, Jasmine decided that death was the only answer to save her sisters. In a delusional state, Jasmine believed she had to kill Carissa and Chloe to protect the younger girls from the men in the house.

The traumatic haze left 15-year-old Jasmine with little memory of shooting Carissa and Chloe. Jasmine was arrested and charged with murder, but found not guilty by reason of temporary insanity. After two years in a mental institution where she earned her GED, Jasmine was released to an adult group home.

The loss of her sisters continued to trouble Jasmine. To fill the hole inside, she got involved in a relationship with a man she thought would love and care for her. Her first two babies were born amidst the dysfunction of drugs and abuse. Jasmine never fought back, believing she deserved the worst for her crime. Jasmine coped by numbing the pain with drugs and alcohol.

The state intervened when Jasmine's third child was born. Social workers took the baby at the hospital, and she received an order to appear in court where she lost her other children.

Enter Jasmine's neighbor Bobbie Jo. She didn't give up when Jasmine refused her multiple invitations to church. Jasmine finally agreed and immediately identified with people at Bridge who spent time in prison before surrendering their lives to Christ.

Jasmine returned the next Sunday.

And the next.

MIRACLES HAPPEN

Twany and I showed Jasmine love despite her past. For three weeks, she sat behind us at church without a clue that we'd once been neighbors. A community outreach event sponsored by several churches sparked the connection when Jasmine invited her mother.

Shock and shame threatened to rock Jasmine's new foundation. People she knew and respected had known her secret.

The very next Sunday Jasmine came to church and confronted my wife and me. "Do you know who I am?"

Twany and I nodded.

"And you allowed me into your church?" Her eyes reflected her disbelief.

"We love you and so does Jesus. He will give you forgiveness and freedom."

Tears spilled from Jasmine's eyes as a weight lifted. The three of us embraced, and the tears flowed.

Jasmine gave her life to Jesus and was baptized at Bridge Church a few weeks later, accepting the forgiveness that only Jesus can offer. After a mission trip to Mexico, Jasmine shared her testimony publically. Today Jasmine is a confident woman and a servant leader at Bridge.

Only God can truly transform a life.

Loving our neighbors is His strategy to change the world. God longs for us to get out of the seats and into the streets.

That's when real miracles happen.

WE ARE BETTER TOGETHER

God has incredible plans for each of us to live life to the fullest and make a difference in our world. Join other readers who are getting out of the seats and into the streets.

Share a story at **www.rondotzler.com** or **www.outoftheseatsandintothestreets.com** about how this book has encouraged you to make a difference in our world. This will encourage all of us to continue to brighten our world.

Be advocates for hope and change, especially for vulnerable children all over the world. God wants to use us to encourage and engage others to provide opportunities for children, youth and adults who would otherwise have no hope.

Consider donating financial resources to "Lights of Hope" at either of the websites above. This foundation was established in memory of Chloe and Carissa. All funds will be used to impact youth and adults in the inner city and around the world.

May God richly bless you as you get out of the seats and into the streets to impact the world for Christ.

Ron Dotzler

ACKNOWLEDGEMENTS

Out of the Seats and Into the Streets is a compilation of stories and insights behind ABIDE's transformational work in inner city Omaha since 1989. ABIDE's impact would not have been possible without the tireless and sacrificial efforts of past and present staff, board members, pastors and thousands of volunteers who have collaboratively shaped the ministry. Your efforts have made this dream come true, and together, we are providing hope to countless lives.

I want to especially thank my wife, Twany, and our fourteen children for stepping out in faith and persevering when all odds seemed stacked against us. Your encouragement, devotion and joyful dispositions have been heart-warming and spirit-lifting. I am so much better because of each of you. I love you.

I want to thank the many family members and friends who have supported and advanced the mission of ABIDE and Bridge. In the early days when I had no idea how to communicate the vision, you stuck by us and helped grow ABIDE and Bridge to what we are today.

For those who were there from the very beginning, your long-term investment, friendship and leadership have made all the difference. I want to thank my parents, Ray and Delores

Dotzler, my siblings and their wives, Ray and Jan Dotzler, Joe and Barb Dotzler and David and Sandi Dotzler, and board members, Rick and Renee Berry and Brad and Julie Knutson. I am so grateful to the leaders of ABIDE and Bridge Church, especially to my son Josh and his wife, Jen, as well as Myron and Kristin Pierce. Your tenacious and innovative leadership has taken ABIDE and Bridge Church to another level. Not only are you leading a movement, this book would have never come to fruition without your love, support and impartation.

A very special thanks to Greg and Nancy Thrasher, Pete and Marilyn Vincentini, Al and Terry Oswald, Chris and Joan Held, Mike Patak, LuAnne Patak, Dean Hodges, Chuck and Judi Downey, John and Wende Kotouc, Bob and Joanne Gjere, Jim Blazek and so many more. I can't begin to express my gratitude to each of you. If ever there is an award for "game-changers," you all would take top prize. When incredible obstacles and challenges faced our city, your faithful commitment to making a difference never subsided. I am humbled by your love, friendship and support.

Thank you to the thousands of volunteers who have worked with children in the inner city or have helped refurbish a Lighthouse. Your efforts have beautified and given hope to our city. I'll forever be grateful to Larry and Barb Welchert and Don and Catherine Stein who shared the vision before ABIDE and Bridge began to take shape. When Twany and I were at our lowest, you were always there. Thank you to the amazing number of influencers, mobilizers, and skilled contractors who have continually worked on projects, shared ideas, involved others, and refurbished Lighthouses and community centers so lives and neighborhoods would be transformed. I want to especially thank, Harry and Pam Tkaczuk, Phil Lorsung, Maxine Lyons, Art and Isabel Martinez, Bob and Jan Drake, George Bang, Lance Brauer, Dick Carpenter, Dan Claxton, Bob and Kathy Laughlin, John and Dodi Imler, Alan Hove, Tom Michaels, Dan Luna and the many more that have contributed to ABIDE and the betterment of our city.

Special pastors in my life have included Elmer Murdoch, Les Beauchamp, Lincoln Murdoch, Ty Schenzel, George and Pam Moore, James and Suzanne Patterson, Jeremiah and Marilyn McGhee, Walter and Melba Hooker, Robert Hall, Bill Bowers, Mark Zhender, Mark Ashton, Craig Walter, Caitlin O'Hare and countless others who are doing incredible work in bringing Christ's kingdom on earth as it is in heaven. I never tire of thanking God for you and telling others of your influence.

And finally, a very special thank you to Shawn Deane, my assistant, and Angela Prusia, the ghostwriter for *Out of the Seats and Into the Streets*. Without your help, the ideas and chapters would not have been as clear or impactful. Words can't express how much you both made this process work.

Thank you everyone.

We truly are better together.

Made in the USA
San Bernardino, CA
10 August 2016